Discovering Welsh History · Book 1

In the Beg

Robert M. Morris & Catrin Stevens

Oxford University Press

J

The publishers would like to thank the following
for permission to reproduce copyright material:

p.6 Science Photo Library; p.7 Science Photo Library; p.8 Biofotos; p.9 *top left, bottom left* Terry Jennings, *bottom right* Viewfinder; p.10 *left* The University Museum, Oxford, *right* Chris Howes; p.11 *top* The University Museum, Oxford, *bottom* National Museum of Wales; p.12 National Museum of Wales; p.13 CM Dixon; p.14 CADW; p.15 CADW; p.17 The University Museum, Oxford; p.18 The British Museum; p.19 Robert Harding Picture Library; p.20 CM Dixon; p.23 *left* National Museum of Wales, *centre left* The British Museum, *right* National Museum of Wales; p.24 *left* Roger Worsley, *right* Mick Sharp; p.25 *top left & right* Roger Worsley, *bottom left & right* John Brennan; p.26 Committee for Aerial Photography, Cambridge University; p.28 The University Museum, Oxford; p.29 CM Dixon; p.31 National Museums of Scotland; p.32 *bottom* The British Library, *top left* National Library of Wales, *top right* CM Dixon; p.37 James Austin; p.43 CADW; p.44 CADW; p.45 *left* CADW, *right* National Museum of Wales; p.46 *top* The British Museum, *centre* Chris Howes, *bottom* Roger Worsley; p.47 *left* National Museum of Wales, *right* Roger Worsley; p.48 Financial Times; p.49 *left* National Museum of Wales, *right* Corinium Museum; p.51 The British Museum; p.52 National Museum of Wales; p.53 *left* National Museum of Wales, *right* Corinium Museum; p.56 CADW; p.57 *top* CADW, *bottom* Arwyn Roberts; p.58 *top* CADW, *bottom* National Museum of Wales; p.59 CADW; p.61 Janet and Colin Bord; p.63 Janet and Colin Bord; p.66 *top* James Pringle, Llanfairpwll, *bottom* Warburg Institute; p.67 *top* Derec Owen, *bottom* National Museum of Wales; p.68 *left* Bodleian Library, *right* Stiftsbibliothek, St. Gallen; p.69 *top* John Brennan, *bottom left* Janet and Colin Bord, *bottom right* CADW; p.70 Tegwyn Roberts; p.71 Cardiff City Council; p.72 *left* Tegwyn Roberts, *right* Y Lolfa; p.75 National Library of Wales; p.76 National Library of Wales; p.77 Wales Tourist Board; p.78 *left* John Brennan, *top right* National Museum of Wales, *bottom right* Janet and Colin Bord; P.80 CM Dixon; p.83 CM Dixon; p.84 Canolfan Hywel Dda, Whitland; p.85 *left* National Library of Wales, *top right* The British Museum, *bottom right* Canolfan Hywel Dda, Whitland; p.86 National Library of Wales; p.87 Margaret Jones, with the kind permission of the Welsh National Centre for Children's Literature; p.88 National Library of Wales; p.89 Canolfan Hywel Dda, Whitland; p.90 National Library of Wales; p.93 National Library of Wales; p.95 National Library of Wales. *Cover photograph* Peter Lord.

Illustrations by G. Caselli, Peter Connolly, Dan Escott, Oliver Frey, Nick Hawken, Richard Hook, Andrew Howat, Margaret Jones, Bernard Long, Angus McBride, Chris Molan and Tony Morris.

Designer and Art Editor: John Brennan, Oxford
Picture Researcher: Rhian Ithel, Cardiff
Research into Welsh prehistory by Philippe Planel

Oxford University Press, Walton Street, Oxford OX2 6DP

Oxford   New York   Toronto
Delhi   Bombay   Calcutta   Madras   Karachi
Kuala Lumpur   Singapore   Hong Kong   Tokyo
Nairobi   Dar es Salaam   Cape Town
Melbourne   Auckland   Madrid

and associated companies in
Berlin and Ibadan

Oxford is a trade mark of Oxford University Press

© Oxford University Press 1991
First published 1991
Reprinted 1993

ISBN 0 19 917138 6

Typeset by MS Filmsetting Limited, Frome, Somerset
Printed in Hong Kong

Contents

C 25000 BC
EARLY STONE AGE
HUNTER-GATHERERS

BURIAL AT
PAVILAND CAVE GOWER

C 5000-2500 BC
NEW STONE/NEOLITHIC AGE

EARLY SETTLERS AND
FARMERS

C 550-700 AD
THE AGE OF SAINTS

C 500 AD THE HEROIC AGE

47AD - 410AD

ST. DAVID AT
LLANDDEWIBREFI

KING ARTHUR
DEFENDS BRITAIN

TOWN LIFE AT CAERWENT

THE EARLY MIDDLE AGES
C 850-1000 AD

942-950 AD

C 750 AD

BUILDING OFFA'S DYKE

THE VIKING RAIDERS

HYWEL DDA -
KING OF WALES

C2400 – 600 BC BRONZE AGE

C600 BC – 47 AD
IRON-AGE CELTS

METALSMITHS MAKING
BRONZE AXES

TOMB-BUILDERS AT
BRYN CELLI DDU

HILLFORTS

IRON-AGE CELTS

R O M A N   W A L E S

47 AD

SOLDIERS AT ISCA

THE ROMANS ARRIVE

CELTIC DRUIDS

T H E   E A R L Y   M I D D L E   A G E S

942 – 1063 AD

C800 – 1063 AD

THE WELSH LAWS –
LAW AND ORDER

A SETTLED FARMING SOCIETY

1

Where is Wales?

Where is Wales? Suppose you were an astronaut looking down from your space module at the earth. Could you find Wales? What shape is it? What other countries are close to it? How would you describe Wales to your mission control? What is the weather like in Wales?

These illustrations might help you. Each one shows Wales getting closer – as if your space module was coming down to land on earth.

From space Wales looks much the same as any other patch of land. If we want to know more about what Wales is like we shall have to take a closer look.

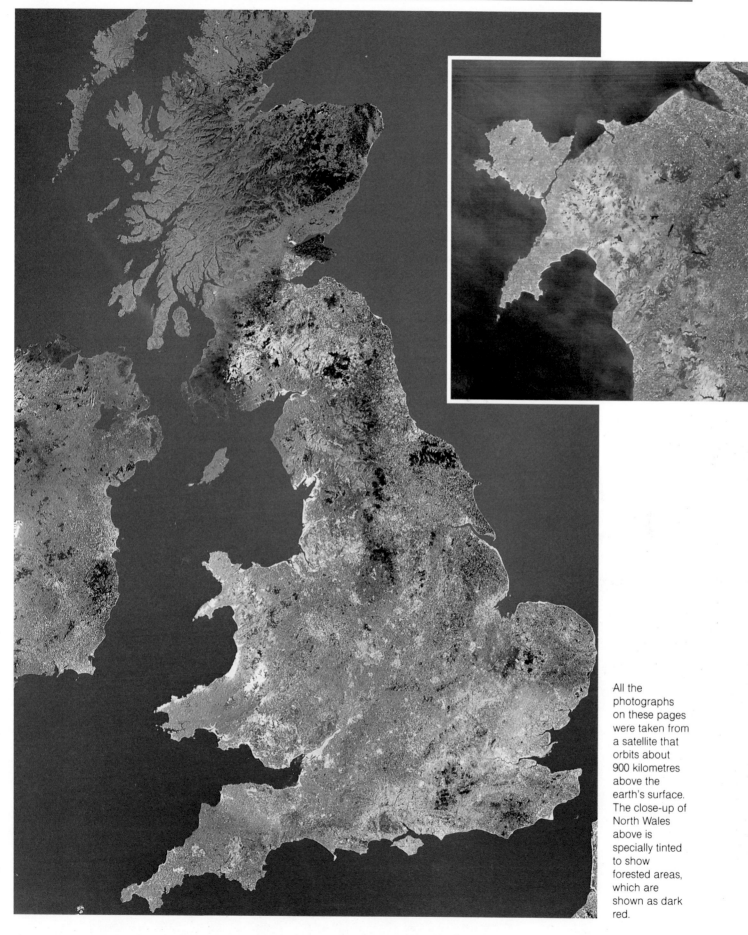

All the photographs on these pages were taken from a satellite that orbits about 900 kilometres above the earth's surface. The close-up of North Wales above is specially tinted to show forested areas, which are shown as dark red.

The Land

The land of Wales is very old. By 'land' we really mean the rocks of which the country is made. Even the soil in your garden and the sand on the beach have come from rocks. If we want to know more, we could ask this man who is looking for fossils in a disused slate quarry at Talysarn, not far from Snowdon.

'Well,' he says, putting down his little hammer, 'rocks themselves, however hard they look, have all been made or formed at some time. Different rocks have been formed in different ways. Take this slate. Millions of years ago it was a sort of clay, but it has been pressed down so hard and for so long that it's turned into these stone-hard sheets. There's a lot of slate in Wales.

'Limestone is another fairly hard rock which has been made in the same way. Did you know that it's composed of the shells and bones of countless millions of tiny sea creatures?

A collection of shells and sea creatures fossilised in limestone

'When they died their tiny bodies drifted down to the bottom of the sea. In time they became covered with thicker and thicker silt which squeezed them down until they became rock.

A fossilised sea lily

'Coal is another example of a rock made in this way but, instead of bones and shells, it's made of the remains of plants that grew on the earth. After tens of millions of years, their life-giving carbon became coal. We've a lot of that in Wales too,' he adds with a smile.

A fern fossilised in coal

'Other rocks have melted and been thrown out over the land as lava by volcanoes, before hardening again. Earthquakes have split the land and made whole mountain blocks slip down to form great valleys in the rock. Ice sheets have covered the land time and time again, and rivers of ice have ripped their way across it, cutting and grinding out deep valleys.

'The different rocks are in layers. Like these slices of slate,' says the geologist, pointing to the slate beds. 'The proper word for a layer is "stratum". If there is more than one, they are called "strata" – Latin words, aren't they?'

We still look a bit puzzled so he takes a sandwich out of his lunch box. 'Take this sandwich,' he says. 'You have a slice of bread, then butter, cheese, butter and bread again – layers, or strata, you see. This sandwich has been cut in half, but the strata are still in the same order and level in both halves. The problem is when the layers get pressed in from both sides. Then they behave in the same way a rug would if you and a friend pushed the edges in towards the middle with your feet. The rug, and of course the layers of rock, buckle up in the centre. That happened to many of the rocks in Wales. Strong rocks stayed in their layers but the whole "sandwich" buckled up to form hills and mountains.

'There are even places where a block of land has split down the middle. In that case, one half of the "sandwich" might end up with its bottom layer level with the top of the other half!'

We leave the geologist to his fossil hunting and stroll on. Remember that all these changes were going on for millions of years before man appeared.

Cemaes Head, Pembrokeshire. An example of folded rocks

9

Paviland Cave

The 'Goat's Hole' is one of two caves in a steep cliff overlooking the sea at Paviland. It is on the western tip of the Gower Peninsula on the South Wales coast. Goat's Hole is not an easy place to get to. There is a steep footpath which climbs from the sea-shore to the caves. A few years ago, some people who were making a film in the cave were cut off by the tide and had to climb down and then swim to safety.

Why should anyone wish to make a film in this gloomy place? What is so special about it? To find out, we'll go back about a hundred and seventy years to 1823.

A man called Dr William Buckland had been staying with friends a few miles from the caves. He was an Oxford professor and an expert on fossils and unusual rocks. He asked some of the local children if they knew any good places to search. They showed him how to climb up to the Goat's Hole. As Buckland scrambled up the steep slope he could not have

The entrance to Paviland Cave today

guessed that he was about to make one of the most exciting discoveries in the history of Wales.

Buckland found the remains of a human skeleton under a pile of stones. The body must have been buried by other humans. The bones were covered in a red substance called ochre and things had been left with the body – bits of bone and flint, beads made from the teeth of a wolf and a pendant of ivory. Buckland thought it was a woman's skeleton. The discovery became known as 'the Red Lady of Paviland'.

There were also other bones in the cave and we now know that they were from animals that had died-out in Wales many thousands of years ago – bear, rhinoceros, elk, hyena, wild horse and woolly mammoth.

Most people in Buckland's time thought that the world was created in 4004 BC and

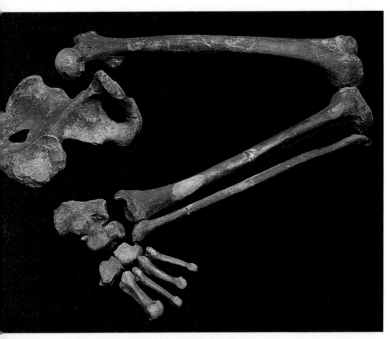

Parts of the skeleton found in Paviland Cave

that there had later been a flood that covered the whole world. Buckland made some important discoveries, but to fit in with the ideas of the time, he suggested the skeleton was from Roman times – much nearer the present – and that the animal bones dated from before the flood. Buckland thought the older animal bones must have been discovered and used by the people carrying out the burial.

Scientists now know that The Red Lady of Paviland was in fact a young man, and the bones have been in the cave for about 25,000 years. The animal bones came from the same time.

There is much that we will never know about the man who was buried in the cave all those years ago. But we do know that he and his people used a range of bone and stone tools, often used in food preparation and the working

of animal skins. These small bands of men, women and children would have always have been on the move, hunting animals and gathering plants, 'hunter-gatherers' we call them. In many ways they were very different from us, but in some ways they showed the same human concerns as we do, making sure that the dead had a proper burial, for example.

An ivory pendant made from a growth in a mammoth's tusk

A Neolithic Family in North Wales

We now move on about 20,000 years from the time of the Paviland burial. A lot has changed. Wales, England and Scotland are now all part of an island. The people of the New Stone Age or Neolithic have settled down, built houses, and started farming. Let's look back.

The weather was hot and the hooves of the oxen move in a low flurry of dust along the hill track. Some villagers are taking their cattle to graze on the higher land for the summer months. The children are glad to leave the fields for the higher pastures – at least they won't have to do any weeding and bird-scaring up there. They can sit and look down on the farm below. How different the small fields and their crops look compared with the uncleared woodland all around.

Some family members have stayed behind

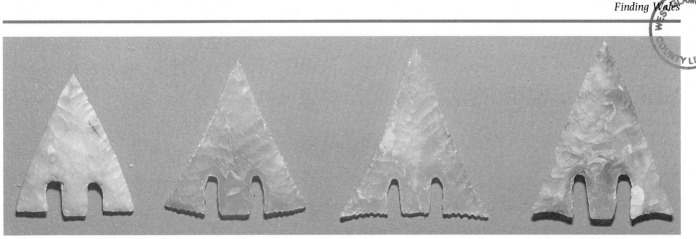
Neolithic arrowheads made from flint

to look after the animals that graze in the lowlands near the farm. The pigs like to root around in the cool of the woodlands close by.

Everyone will be back at the farm in time for the harvest. This is also the time to kill an animal and offer it in thanks to the spirits for the year that had gone by, and also make sure that there will be enough food throughout the coming winter.

These farmers and their children aren't just good at growing crops, they can weave clothes with wool from the sheep, make pottery on open fires, manufacture and polish stone axes, and carve all sorts of useful and decorative objects from wood and bone. Nor have they forgotten the hunting and fishing skills of their ancestors. They often bring back red deer, wild boar, wild cat, beaver, hare, even brown bear and wolf. They also go fishing, picking blackcurrants, sloes, crab apples and hazel nuts on the way. Quite a larder in some seasons, but the winter can be terrible. The eldest and youngest often die in winter.

We know that families lived like this in Wales in Neolithic times because archaeologists (people who look at what the past has left behind) have found the remains of farming activity – at Gwernvale, near Abergavenny, for example. In some areas archaeologists have been lucky enough to find wooden objects that have been protected by the type of ground they were in. At Llandygái in North Wales, the remains of a building were found and also a rubbish dump with broken pots, flint tools and animal bones.

A finely decorated Neolithic beaker

Neolithic arrowheads, spearheads and a polished stone axe

The Tomb Builders

Bryn Celli Ddu, a passage grave in Anglesey

As well as farming, neolithic people also built a whole range of monuments in earth and stone. We are still surprised today at the organisation and team work needed to build these monuments and the amount of time people must have taken from their work in the fields to drag huge stones and move tons of earth. The tools they used were very basic, such as pick axes made from deer antlers. Archaeologists are still trying to find out more about why these monuments and tombs may have been built.

If you cross one of the two high bridges that span the Menai Straits to Anglesey you can visit a number of stone monuments from our distant past. Many of these were graves. One of them is called Bryn Celli Ddu – 'The Hill of the Dark Wood'. It sounds brooding and mysterious!

Bryn Celli Ddu was a 'passage grave' – a corridor of large stone slabs with other heavy stones across the top. Smaller stones filled in the gaps and the whole thing was covered over with earth. Many bodies were buried inside it over the years, important people probably.

The bodies may have been burned first, or even laid out on platforms for some time before they were buried, as is still done in some parts of the world today.

The interesting thing about Bryn Celli Ddu is that the passage grave is built on top of an earlier monument called a 'henge' – like Stonehenge. The henge was quite violently destroyed when the passage grave was built. Imagine that we are going back about four

14

thousand years to when the passage grave was being built. Let's see what is happening.

A large group of people is waiting around the stones of the meeting place by the river. On the inside of a round ditch there is a circle of stones. In the centre of the circle is a freshly dug pit, over a metre deep. One of the men is laying a small bone and some wood among the smoking ashes of a recent fire. At the edge of the pit is a stone covered with carvings. The rest of the people chant in low, droning voices as the priest goes on with this strange ceremony.

There's an old man standing a short distance away, half hidden behind a tree. Let's ask him what has been going on.

'I'm an outcast so they won't let me take part, but I've kept a close eye on what's been going on. All these comings and goings from the land across the sea. They're going to destroy the old meeting place and build a big stone grave in the middle. It will take the work of all our people to build the mound over the top, they will come from far and wide. They are all afraid of the power of the old meeting place. Look, they are starting to break up the old stones. They're knocking over the stones and dropping other stones on top of them.'

The inner passage leading to the chamber of Bryn Celli Ddu

Quarrymen, Miners, Carvers and Smiths

Throughout prehistory (that is, right up to the time of the Romans) we know that people in Wales made more and more use of the natural world around them to make beautiful objects from stone, bone, wood and metal. They made tools, weapons, ornaments and even musical instruments.

Back in the time of the first farmers, stone axeheads from North Wales were given or traded to people many hundreds of miles away. There are quarry sites where the axes were roughly made before they were taken away to be finished and polished.

At around the time the passage grave of Bryn Celli Ddu was built, a new material

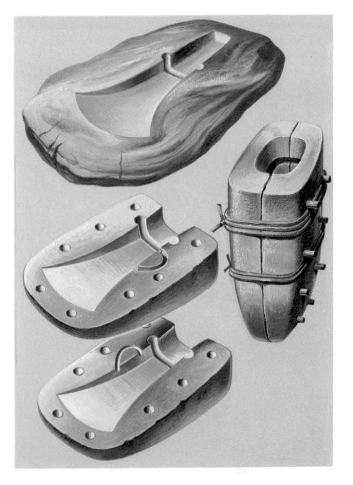

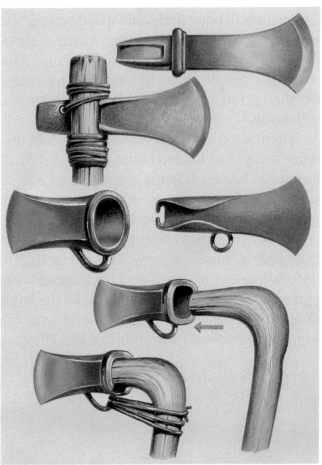

Metalsmiths first worked with open moulds. Simple shapes were carved out of soft stone. Molten bronze was poured into the moulds and allowed to cool. Later moulds were made in two halves. Solid axeheads were mounted in wooden shafts. When the metalsmiths became more skilled they were able to make axeheads with sockets into which the wooden shaft could be firmly fixed.

became known. This was the metal copper. People found that if they mixed copper with small amounts of another metal, like tin, they could make a much stronger metal called bronze. Stone tools were still made, but the most valuable objects were now made of bronze. Metalsmiths became very important people.

Cuch was lucky. He was going to start work with the metal smith. The smith was about the only person who didn't work in the fields. His skill with metal was more useful than his skill with a plough. The chief was always in the best of moods when he saw the newly produced bronze axeheads. He used them to pay back favours, he exchanged them for other goods, or to keep people on his side. He knew that having one of the best smiths in the land made him very important. The chief made sure that the smith and his family had everything they needed.

Cuch was looking forward to the long journey to the mines where the coloured rocks from which the metal came were mined. He would help look after the furnace where the rocks were melted down. He would have to spend hours at a time working the bellows to keep the heat up, and adding more fuel. Sometimes he would have to work on through the night. Bringing in all the wood needed for furnace would be less exciting, but he wasn't going to complain.

Cuch had been told that if he worked well, and he meant to, he would one day help with the most difficult work, like making the moulds into which the molten metal would flow, or working sheets of metal. Cuch had been chosen because everyone knew he was very good at carving wood. Of course his family was related to smith's family, some jealous tongues say that may have helped!

A moulded bronze axehead

2

The Celts

Who were the Celts?

We are now in the last thousand years of prehistory before the birth of Christ. There are many changes, in Wales and elsewhere. To begin with people are now using a new metal – iron. Tools and weapons are made from iron. There are new fashions in jewellery and decoration. Horse riding and wheeled carts and chariots have become more common. All these changes are linked to the appearance of a new people in Wales, called the Celts. They have brought with them their own language and habits.

The problem for archaeologists is that it is difficult to tell when the Celts arrived. Some of the objects that they used may already have arrived in Wales before the Celtic people. We don't even know if the Celts came in large numbers at any one time. Suppose that an archaeologist of the future was looking at the way we live today, he or she would find a lot of evidence of Japanese cars and other Japanese goods. Would this mean that the Japanese had invaded the country?

This is a model of a man who died over 2000 years ago. His body was found in Lindow Moss in Cheshire in 1984 and scientists were able to base this model of his head on the remains found in the bog.

Fortunately we do know a bit more about the Celts. For one thing their language has survived. Also, although the Celts didn't write things down, they came into contact with people who did, the Greeks and Romans. The Celts were creating quite a stir in Europe, people were interested in them. If you read what Greek historians have said about them you will see why.

'The whole race is madly fond of war, high spirited and quick to battle, but otherwise straightforward and not of evil character.

Some shave off the beard, whilst others cultivate a short beard; the nobles shave the cheeks but let the moustache grow freely so that it covers the mouth. And so when they are eating the moustache becomes entangled in the food, and when they drink the drink passes, as it were, through a sort of strainer. When dining they all sit not on chairs, but on the earth, strewing beneath them the skins of wolves or dogs. Beside them are hearths blazing with fire, with cauldrons and spits containing large pieces of meat.

They wear a striking form of clothing – tunics died and stained in various colours, and trousers, which they call by the name of bracae; and they wear striped cloaks, fastened with buckles, thick in winter and light in summer, picked out with a variegated small check pattern. They are terrifying in appearance, with deep-sounding and very harsh voices. In conversation they use few words and speak in riddles, for the most part hinting at things and leaving a great deal to be understood.

To the frankness and high-spiritedness of their temperament must be added childish boastfulness and love of decoration. They wear ornaments of gold, torcs on their necks and bracelets on their arms and wrists. It is this vanity which makes them unbearable in victory and so downcast in defeat. They possess a trait of barbarous savagery which is especially common to the northern peoples, for when they leave the battlefield they fasten to the necks of their horses the heads of their enemies, and on arriving home they nail up this spectacle at the entrances of their houses'.

The head of an Iron Age man found preserved in a peat-bog in Tollund, Denmark

2

A People Grow Up

Where did the Celts come from? Some scientists think that their original homeland was in the upper Danube valley in parts of modern Bohemia, Hungary, Bavaria and Austria. Their ancestors may have been the people who buried their dead in pottery vessels and are known as 'The Urn Folk'.

Those who lived in Austria probably grew rich because they controlled the supplies of salt from nearby mines. Salt was highly valued by everyone in those days, for cooking and for preserving meat and fish. At a place called Hallstatt, near Salzburg, many Celtic remains were found – cauldrons, swords, horse-harness pieces and other items.

The Celts had been skilled bronzesmiths.

Above A gold torc found in Norfolk
Right Stages in the process of making iron swords

When they discovered how to make useful and decorative objects out of iron, they had something other than salt to trade. Their traders carried goods down river valleys or along hill ridge paths. In return they received things such as pottery, silk, and gold. They were good potters themselves, and they also made beautiful jewellery from both bronze and gold. The torcs they wore round their necks were fashioned from twisted gold wire.

As the years went by, the Celtic tribes began to expand. They looked for new lands to feed their growing populations. Their iron swords and spears and their mastery of horse-drawn chariots made them difficult to stop. In the west they pushed through Germany and into Gaul (modern France), and eventually across the Pyrenees into Spain and Portugal. In north-west Spain is an area known as 'Galicia' – a Spanish form of 'Celt'.

Greeks sacked and burnt Rome in 390 BC, and attacked the famous Greek shrine at Delphi in 279 BC. Shortly after the Delphi attack, a group of them settled in what is now Turkey. By 250 BC there was a broad band of Celtic tribes right across Europe from Ireland and Spain to Turkey.

The Celts first arrived in Britain about 500 BC. They reached Wales by about 400 BC. In less than a century they had occupied practically the whole of mainland Britain.

The movement of Celtic people from Central Europe

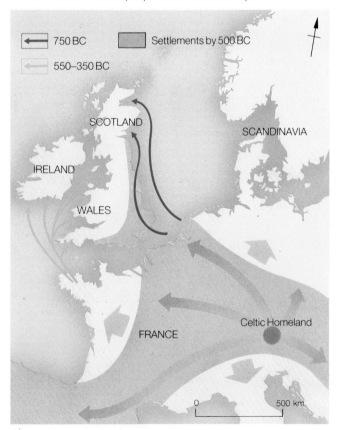

← 750 BC	Settlements by 500 BC
← 550–350 BC	

SCOTLAND

SCANDINAVIA

IRELAND

WALES

Celtic Homeland

FRANCE

0   500 km

The Celts rarely lived in large towns but they did have large heavily defended forts which they built on the tops of hills. They were crop farmers and herdsmen but their warriors spent much of their time breeding and raising horses. Sheep were kept for their wool which was woven into cloth.

When a tribe was ready to move, belongings were loaded on to pack animals or into rough carts; the sheep, cattle and horses were rounded up into herds and the warriors set off on horseback or drove away in their chariots. Their task was to make sure the way was safe for their families.

21

The Secret of the Lake

The Royal Air Force base at Valley, in Anglesey, stands near the shore. It is on flat, sandy ground with streams, lakes and marshes close by. In 1942 workmen were building a new landing strip for the base. It was during the Second World War, and the work had to be done quickly. The men were digging thick, black peat out of the ground. As they spread the peat out they found a length of iron chain and some other objects. As it happened they needed a chain and used it to tow a lorry which had stuck in the mud.

'Where did this come from?' asked Mr Jones, the engineer in charge, pointing to the chain.

'From the marsh by the lake at Llyn Cerrig Bach', said the lorry driver, 'and there were other things'.

Mr Jones gave instructions that all the iron bits and pieces should be rescued and collected. He had a suspicion that they were old – very old indeed.

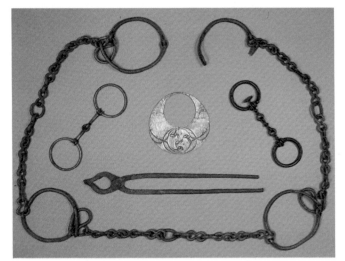

A piece of the chain and other artefacts from Llyn Cerrig Bach

Soon Mr Jones was writing a letter to Sir Cyril Fox, the head of the National Museum of Wales in Cardiff. Sir Cyril was used to digging up or dealing with very old objects; he was a well known archaeologist. He came up to Valley and looked carefully around Llyn Cerrig Bach.

'I think this marsh was once part of the lake', he told Mr Jones. 'All the things you've found were probably thrown into the lake.'

'How long ago?' asked Mr Jones.

'In the Iron Age – possibly two thousand years .'

'But why did they throw good stuff away?' Mr Jones was a practical man.

'It was an offering – a gift to the gods. These people thought the gods could be pleased by giving them presents like these. Sometimes sacrifices may have been offered.'

Mr Jones remembered the way the ancient chain had stood up to the weight of a lorry. 'Superstitious or whatever else they were, they were fine craftsmen.'

Fine craftsmen – Sir Cyril turned these words over in his mind as he made the long train journey back to Cardiff. Some time later he went to the industrial town of Pontypridd

and showed the chain to two expert chain-makers, the Richardson brothers, at the Brown Lennox and Company's works. He told them how it had been found and asked them what they could tell him about it. They told him that it had been made in a very similar way to modern chains. Each link was closed by squeezing it in the middle while the iron was still red-hot. This made the link stronger and stopped it twisting. You can see this if you look at the picture of the chain.

The Richardsons wanted to know what it had been used for.

'It was a gang chain', replied Sir Cyril. 'It was used to chain prisoners or slaves together. The large rings were clamped round the prisoners' necks.'

'Who made it?'

'Iron Age people – although perhaps not in Anglesey. Some of the things could have been taken to Anglesey by traders. But the craftsmen who made the chain and the folk who threw it into Llyn Cerrig Bach had a lot in common.'

Many other objects came from Llyn Cerrig Bach including portions of trumpets and cauldrons, all showing typical Celtic workmanship. Perhaps the most exciting was the remains of a war chariot. You can see a reconstruction of it in the National Museum of Wales in Cardiff.

A model of the war chariot that was found in Llyn Cerrig Bach

Finding Out About the Celts

It was going to be a different sort of lesson today. Mr Williams had invited an archaeologist, Mrs Vaughan, to come into school and answer questions on how an archaeologist works and how she knows about the way people used to live before the Roman conquest of Wales. The archaeologist explained that her job was to look at what had actually survived from the past, and that for thousands of years of Welsh history this was the only way of finding out, because nothing had been written down. She then talked about the people of the Celtic Iron Age, the houses they built, the tools and weapons they used, the clothes they probably wore. She asked the class if there were any questions. A forest of hands shot up, but Eleri was first.

'*How do you know they were farmers, miss?*'

'Well', replied Mrs Vaughan, 'to begin with food was very hard to grow in those days, and everyone except chiefs, priests and a few warriors and craftsmen had to grow food, so they were nearly all farmers'.

'*They could have gone hunting and fishing*', someone suggested.

'Yes, and they probably did' agreed Mrs Vaughan, 'but they couldn't rely on hunting and fishing for all their needs, like their ancestors. They weren't on the move all the time – there were too many people by then. A few years ago part of an early plough, an ard, was found in an Iron Age settlement. We sometimes also find ploughmarks in the small fields we think the Celts used'.

'*Is that the only way we know they were farmers?*', asked Glyn.

Archaeologists at work at the Walesland Rath site

A saddle quern used for grinding grain

'I can see that you really want to get to the heart of the matter! There are other ways we can tell. For example, we find small hand grinding mills, called querns, for making flour, and you don't need querns if you don't grow grain. We also find the grain itself, usually half burnt – that's how it survives – sometimes accidentally pressed into pottery'.

'*What else lasts to modern times?*', asks someone else.

'That's a good question. We find the outlines of houses, banks, ditches and roadways. Sometimes the soil is just a different colour; it could be the stain that rotted wood leaves behind. We also find artefacts (objects), especially metal, stone and pottery. Then, of course,

we find bones. All these things help build up a picture of how people lived. What would bones tell us?'

'*How healthy people were ... whether they died in a fight*', answers Sian, slightly surprised at her own good idea.

'Yes, and in the case of animal bones, we can even tell at what age animals were being killed for food and which cuts of meat were popular, which brings us back to farming'.

'*Well*', said Mr Williams, '*to think all of these things might be under our very feet*'.

'*What about fighting*', asks Iwan.

'Sometimes hillfort defences are found to have collapsed, because the timbers were burnt, which is unlikely to have been an accident. Hillforts were definitely attacked. Ammunition dumps, piles of smooth stones, are sometimes found inside hillforts, but there must have been a good deal of bragging and parading as well as fighting. Some of the finest and most decorated Celtic weapons were probably mainly for show and not for fighting at all.'

The outline of a large circular hut can be seen here. The buckets are used to collect soil which is then sieved to find smaller items

Often the only evidence that remains of a building is of postholes like this one into which posts used to be fixed. The posts themselves rotted away long ago

The class were beginning to see the Celts in their mind's eye. It isn't easy to picture people living in the same area as yourself but living in a completely different way – no television, hospitals, shops, cars. No comfort save that provided by the fire and the stew in the boiling cauldron. No entertainment except the songs, stories and dances of the people you know around you.

2

Hillforts

People in Wales at the time of the Celts obviously felt they needed to defend themselves against attack. These were troubled times. Even quite small settlements were defended, and those farmsteads which were not defended often lay in the protective shadow of a large hillfort.

Tre'r Ceiri, a hillfort in Gwynedd

Angus McBride

Today these hillforts seem very cold and windy places to live. In fact they may only have been used when attacks were feared. The hillfort builders used the natural strength of a hilltop, adding stone walls as an extra defence. Sometimes the stone walls were laced with timber for extra strength. The gates could be the weakest link in the defences so the builders often took special care to make the main entrances strong. These hillforts were used by the Celts at least until the Romans arrived in Wales.

It is not hard to see why the Celts built strong forts in many parts of Wales. A tribe that was defending a hillfort had an advantage over the attacking warriors. It was harder to attack uphill. The defenders could throw stones at their attackers and once an enemy reached the outer walls they were met by long spears.

All the same, many hillforts were taken by the attackers who then took the defenders captive. All the younger men and women would be made slaves and carried away to serve their new masters. No wonder the young boys of the tribe trained and worked so hard to become fine warriors!

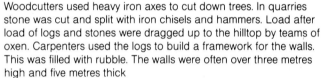

Woodcutters used heavy iron axes to cut down trees. In quarries stone was cut and split with iron chisels and hammers. Load after load of logs and stones were dragged up to the hilltop by teams of oxen. Carpenters used the logs to build a framework for the walls. This was filled with rubble. The walls were often over three metres high and five metres thick

A Warrior Returns Home

A Celtic brooch

In some parts of Wales there were no large hillforts in the Celtic Iron Age. In these areas archaeologists think that people lived in smaller defended settlements. One of these settlements, the Walesland Rath (Dyfed), has been found and excavated. Let's go back now to one of these settlements late on a winter's day in the first century BC.

The fields around the village have already been ploughed to let the winter frosts break down the clods of soil. As soon as the cold weather is over, the oats, barley and wheat will be sown. By the summer the seeds will have grown into tall plants swaying in the breeze. The fields are small, no more than a man can plough in one day. Now they are empty.

Brân hesitates as the banks that protect the settlement come into view. He can see the thatch of the huts and the smoke from the fires inside them rising lazily in the fading afternoon light. Some of the farm animals are still outside the banks and a few children are returning with water from the nearby river. It is not going to be a hero's return for Brân, so he decides to wait until everyone gathers around the fires later on before making his entrance. He feels foolish enough returning from a cattle raid without any cattle, but to return without his horse either is too much!

Brân is wearing a heavy woollen cloak over his shoulders, made by his sisters and his mother, which is fastened at the collar with a fine brooch. Underneath he's in full battle dress. His skin is covered in the blue dye of the woad plant. They had laughed enough when he had prepared himself: 'Why are you wearing woad for a night raid?' Brân thought that the small farm over the hills would not expect cattle raiders at this cold time of year, when the beasts were kept close by the farm. Everyone would be asleep. He thought he could handle the dogs; that had been his mistake. Why did they have to make so much noise, and wake up everyone for miles around?

Brân shakes himself, he has waited long enough and the gates of the settlement are now closed. He tries to put a swing into his step as his cousin on the tower recognises him approaching through the dusk.

'What happened?'

Brân does not reply. The gates swing open and he makes his way across the cobbled entrance, past the round huts to the elder's hut.

Until his eyes are used to the darkness of the hut Brân can see nothing except the shape of the bottom of the cauldron over the embers of the fire. He knows the elder will be the first to speak. The voice comes from the back of the hut.

'So, Brân returns more quietly than when he left. We expected to hear the sound of many hooves over the cobbles this evening.'

There's the sound of muffled laughter, but the elder continues:

'Draw from the cauldron Brân; tomorrow you and your brothers and sisters will be clearing the new fields, I will come and speak to you then.'

The elder is a fair man.

After Brân has had a little to eat and listened to one or two of the bard's tales, he returns to his hut. His family have heard he's back and are glad he's safely home. Brân is still hungry and thirsty. He drinks from his wooden bowl and eats some oatcakes and cheese before he lies down on his bed of leaves, and covers himself with his cloak and his fleece. There will be plenty to do tomorrow and other chances to prove himself as a warrior.

A Celtic shield

2

Daily Life of the Celts

Not all the time was taken up fighting other tribes. There were sometimes long periods of peace when the life of the tribe passed quietly.

Celtic families lived in round houses. The walls were made of wood or of reeds and hardened mud and the roof was made of reeds or straw.

Life must have been a bit crowded in a Celtic round house. The children slept on the floor, usually on piles of heather or bracken. Their mother and father slept on a pair of wooden benches covered with old animal skins. In the centre of the hut a large fire was kept burning all the time. It would have been nice and warm inside, but very smoky.

Usually there was enough to eat – meat

man could often plough a field in a single day. Then there were the animals to look after. In the summer the animals were taken to the hilly areas to feed. The rich pastures close to home were saved for later in the year, or times of trouble. There were also the fields of corn and oats. Everything depended on a good harvest.

There was certainly a lot of work for the women to do. Apart from working in the fields, caring for the animals, cooking food, and looking after the family, they also had to make all the clothes. First, the wool had to be combed, using a bone comb. Then it was spun into fine threads and woven into beautiful cloth. The Celts particularly liked colourful clothes.

Today we buy most of the things we need, particularly food and clothes. Imagine how hard life must have been when everything had to be done or made in the home.

The remains of a piece of woven cloth

A bone comb used by weavers

from the sheep or cattle which they kept, or from the wild animals they hunted. There were oat-cakes made from crops grown in the fields, and in autumn there were fruits and wild berries. The hardest times were the cold months of the new year and early spring. The family had to rely for food on what was left from the last season. When the snow fell and the nights were long everyone gathered around the fire to listen to the old folk telling stories of the tribe's history, its heroes, battles, victories and glory.

The family looked forward to the warmer weather. Then everybody had plenty of work to do.

The Celts were really good farmers. In the spring-time the men of the tribe would be working the fields, walking behind their oxen and plough. The fields were not too large and a

The Druids

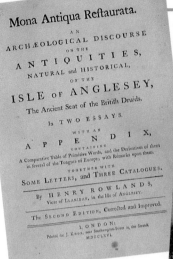

The title page of Rowlands' book, and St Seiriol's Well at Penmon, Anglesey. The well is believed to be an ancient Druidic spring.

Henry Rowlands was vicar of Llanidan in Anglesey during the early 1700s. As well as being a good priest, Henry was very interested in the local legends and the history of the island where he lived. He had seen the ruins of old huts and forts as well as a strange group of stones in the open fields and he did his best to find out about them.

As an educated man, Henry had learnt Latin and was able to read Julius Caesar's account of his conquests. Caesar mentioned the Celtic priests, or druids. Henry had also read a history of the conquest of Britain, written by the Roman historian, Tacitus. The Romans had been determined to find the druids and destroy them. Suetonius Paulinus had tried to do this in the year AD 61, with some success, but the revolt by the famous Celtic leader Boudicca in the east of Britain had called him back from Wales. It was a quarter of

a century later before Anglesey, and the rest of North Wales, was finally overrun by soldiers commanded by Julius Agricola. Tacitus praised Agricola's good leadership – hardly surprising since Tacitus was the Roman commander's son-in-law!

Henry Rowlands became more and more interested in the druids. After reading a lot about them, he came to the conclusion that the druids were responsible for building all the stone circles such as Stonehenge, all the boulder tombs and all the standing stones on his own Anglesey. He thought they had great and mysterious powers. He even wrote a book about the druids, full of pictures showing what he thought they were like.

Archaeologists now know that Henry Rowlands was wrong about what the druids built – his local stones, the stone circles and barrows were all very much older than the druids. However, we still don't know as much about these people as we'd like. Let's imagine that we have been transported back in time to a meeting led by the druids.

There are people wrapped in woollen cloaks coming through the woods. It is a gloomy autumn day with a thin drizzle of rain. The people have left their homes and smoky wood fires for an important ceremony. The druids are going to make a sacrifice to the gods. Only the druids know the secrets of the gods

An early 19th century picture of a druid, showing the popular idea at the time of what druids were like

and how to please them. If the gods are happy the crops will grow well and the folds will be full of sheep. The druids also know when the gods are angry and must be calmed by offering them a gift that the tribe values – iron, or gold, or even a life.

Animals were frequently sacrificed and sometimes people were, too. Once, a king was killed as an offering to the gods because he had grown too old to lead his warriors into battle!

Sacrifices were held far away from places where people lived. A lonely clearing in a wood was a good place, particularly if there were oak trees with mistletoe growing on them. The druids believed that mistletoe had magic powers and used to cut it down with a golden sickle, catching it as it fell in a snow-white cloth. People chosen for sacrifice would often be given some of the magic berries beforehand to dull their senses. Victims might be burned, stabbed, strangled, shot with arrows or

drowned. The body might then be buried in a convenient peat bog.

The druids were the wise men of the tribe. They advised the king on important matters. They knew about the length of the year and the change in the seasons – this was very important for the farmers. They had explanations for everything from lightning strikes to eclipses of the moon. The gods ruled the forces of nature, so it was in everyone's interest to keep them happy. Only the druids knew how to do this, for they alone understood the gods and their moods. What a pity they didn't write down some of their secrets. Perhaps if they had done so, people like Henry Rowlands wouldn't have had to imagine quite so much!

Druids had to remember all the words of their ceremonies and all the laws of their tribe because they were forbidden to write anything down. It's possible that these things were learnt more easily by being set out as rhymes.

The Romans are Coming!

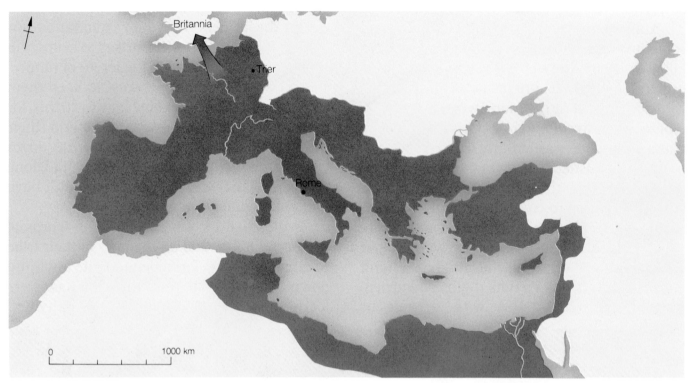

The extent of the Roman Empire (coloured red) in AD 43

The great city of Rome had started as nothing more than a small village settlement on a group of hills in Italy. It had grown to be a town and, after a long while, a powerful nation. As Rome grew larger its soldiers started to conquer the lands nearby until, some centuries later, Rome ruled all of Italy. Later still, the legionaries, as Rome's soldiers were called, overran all the lands around the Mediterranean. Rome became the largest empire the world had seen. In AD 43 Rome began to conquer Britain.

Claudius Caesar, Rome's emperor, knew something of Britain. Almost one hundred years earlier Julius Caesar, a great Roman general, had attacked Britain. He had written a book about his wars with the Celts. Claudius knew that many British tribes sent corn, leather and wool to Rome in exchange for fine pottery and wine. Roman traders also brought tin and gold from Britain.

The Roman armies landed in Kent and began to battle against the Celtic warriors of south-east England. There was some fierce fighting. The Celtic chieftain, Caradog, or Caratacus as the Romans called him, was beaten by the legions and fled to Wales to warn the tribes there of the danger that threatened them.

The glittering helmets, breast armour and spears of the legionaries were seen further and further from Kent as the invading legions advanced north and west. At last, around AD 47, the legions reached Wales and under their general, Ostorius Scapula, they began to attack the Welsh Celts.

In those days there were four main tribes in Wales – the Silures (mostly in modern Gwent and Glamorgan), the Demetae (to the west of the Silures and in modern Dyfed), the Ordovices (mainly central Wales and the north-west) and finally the Deceangli (in modern Clwyd).

Caradog organised the Silures of South Wales into a tough fighting force. They won many minor victories against the Romans and always avoided a full-scale battle. The Romans

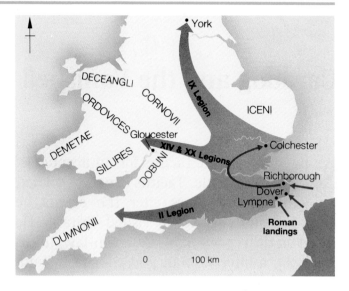

set up a powerful legionary fort at the edge of Silurian territory, from which they could attack Caradog. The Romans called it Glevum – we know it as Gloucester.

Tacitus, a Roman historian, tells us that the Silures under Caradog harassed and worried the legions for almost eight years along the frontier between what the Romans had taken and what they hadn't. The Silures were helped in their struggles by the Ordovices to the north.

The story of Caradog's last battle is told on the next page.

3

Caradog and the Vanished Battlefield

We have to rely on Tacitus for an account of Caradog's last battle. Tacitus wasn't a soldier, he wrote many years after the events he described and he never visited Britain. He relied on the reports of his father-in-law, Julius Agricola, a later Roman governor of Britain. For these reasons, it's sometimes hard for us to identify the site of the battle he wrote about. Tacitus gives no names, only vague descriptions.

It was in or about the year AD 51 when Caradog decided to give up lightning raids and ambushes and to risk a pitched battle. We think it was in mid Wales, somewhere on the River Severn. See if you can pick out any clues as to the kind of place it was from this description written by Tacitus.

'The natural fierceness of the people was made stronger by their belief in the ability of Caratacus. He made up for the smallness of his army by being more cunning and knowing the land well. Moving the war to the land of the Ordovices, he was joined by everyone who feared a Roman peace. Then Caratacus took a gamble and chanced a battle. He chose a site where many things (especially the difficulty of the approach roads and the escape routes) helped him and hindered the legions. On one side there were steep hills and overhanging cliffs. Wherever the slope was gentler, stones were piled up to make a kind of rampart. In front of him was a river with no fords or easy crossing places. There were plenty of men at these defences.'

Caradog hurried from one point to the next encouraging his warriors and telling them that this was the day and the battle which would either win them back their freedom or make them slaves for ever.

The high spirits of the Welsh Celts dismayed the Roman commander. He was already worried by the tall cliffs, the river barrier and the stone rampart. But the legionaries, cheered on by their officers, shouted for battle, saying that bravery could overcome anything. Their officers told them the same thing and sent small parties of men forward to look for weak points.

Somehow or other the legions managed to cross the river and tried to storm the rampart, but the Celts drove them back with arrows and sling stones. A second attempt was made with the Romans locking shields and advancing behind this moving wall. At last they got over the rampart and then, in close formation, they drove their enemy back at sword point.

Lightly-armed Roman auxiliary soldiers threw showers of javelins from one side of the battlefield. The armoured legionaries advanced in a solid, disciplined line. The Celts were thrown into disorder. Those who were not killed in the battle melted away down the mountain paths Caradog had picked out.

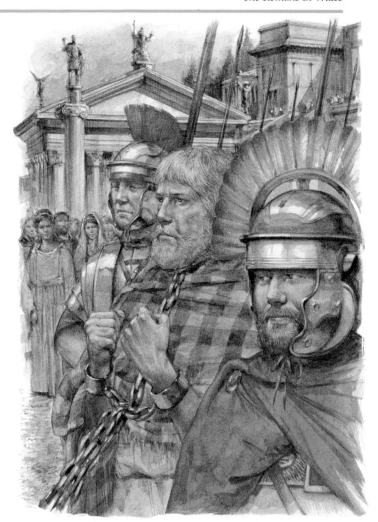

The ruins of the Imperial Forum in Rome

Caradog himself was captured at last and taken to Rome in chains. According to Tacitus, he said, 'If I had been only a little more successful you would have welcomed me as a king, not as a captive. I had an army, men and horses. Are you surprised that I am sorry that you have taken them from me? Of course, you want to rule the world but you can't expect those whom you have conquered to rejoice as you do in your own success.'

Another and rather touching version has Caradog saying, as he looked at Rome's huge and magnificent marble buildings, 'If you had all these fine temples and palaces, why did you want my little mud hut?'

Whatever he said, his bearing and bravery so impressed the emperor that the Celt, together with his wife and family, were released from their chains and given a pension to live out their lonely lives in Rome.

Suetonius Paulinus and the End of the Druids

Tacitus also wrote about how the Romans conquered the island of Mona, Anglesey or Ynys Môn today. This time the Roman commander was Suetonius Paulinus. The invasion began in AD 60, nine years after the defeat of Caradog. The Romans had not got much further into Wales and it's likely that they thought the druids were encouraging the Celtic tribes to resist from their stronghold on the island.

Anglesey was a fertile area which could supply food to the Ordovices, still resisting in the mountains, where little would grow. The Romans therefore decided to smash the druids and cut off supplies to the Ordovices. This is the story that Tacitus told:

1. Mona was a fertile island full of people who had gone there from other parts of Wales for safety's sake.

2. The sea between the mainland and the island is called the Menai Straits. It is shallow but dangerous.

3. Suetonius Paulinus's soldiers built a fleet of flat-bottomed boats in which they could cross.

4. The cavalrymen followed on horseback, swimming when the water got too deep.

5. Before them on the shoreline stood the enemy in threatening lines.

6. Among the warriors were black-robed women with dishevelled hair, looking like the Furies (Roman goddesses of revenge) and waving flaming torches.

7. Nearby, a group of white-clad druids were raising their hands to the sky and screaming dreadful curses.

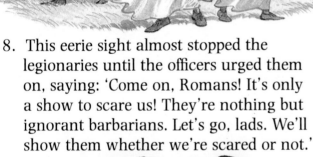

8. This eerie sight almost stopped the legionaries until the officers urged them on, saying: 'Come on, Romans! It's only a show to scare us! They're nothing but ignorant barbarians. Let's go, lads. We'll show them whether we're scared or not.'

9. The legionaries charged forward behind their eagle.

10. They beat the enemy and dispersed them: many (including a large number of druids) were killed. The Romans destroyed the sacred groves of trees used by the druids for their savage and superstitious ceremonies.

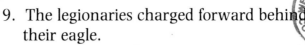

Suetonius Paulinus did not have time to celebrate his victory over the druids. News came of a great Celtic revolt in the east of Britain. In AD 61, he had to leave Wales in order to fight Boudicca.

The Making of a Roman Fort

It is the year AD 75 – just over thirty years since the Romans began their invasion of Britain. We are a few miles upstream on the River Usk in south Wales. Roman legionary working parties are grubbing up bushes and using oxen to haul out tree stumps. They are clearing the area so that a legionary fortress can be built.

The surveyor is working out exactly where the various buildings in the fort will go. He is using a 'groma', a Roman surveying instrument. It helps him set out right-angles for the corners of the four walls and for the buildings inside.

His assistants mark out the lines and the outside measurements of the fort are scratched into the soil and marked with pegs and poles. Other poles show where the gates are to be. There is a gate in the middle of each of the four walls. Main roads will run between opposite pairs of gates.

The men who have been measuring the site of the walls with a ten foot ruler, marked off in 'pedes' or 'feet', move to the spot where the main roads will cross in the middle of the camp. They begin to mark out the area where the headquarters building will be.

Now the centurion in charge sends a large party of soldiers to dig the main ditch. It runs along the line of the walls and the men pile up the earth to form a rampart. A temporary wooden fence is built on top of the rampart. Later it will be replaced with a stone wall. Another working group has already started to build the commander's house.

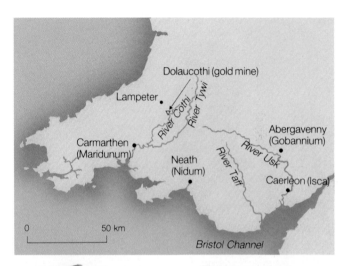

A Roman soldier carried all his equipment with him: **1** Forked or T-pole to which most loose kit was tied. **2** Bronze bucket or cook-pot. **3** Pickaxe for rampart digging. **4** Bag for cloak, personal possessions, cleaning kit, etc. **5** Reinforced satchel, probably for tools – saws, chain, sickle and rope, and perhaps spare thongs, buckles, etc. **6** Leather shield-cover. **7** Two wooden stakes, added to others in fence along top of camp rampart and tied together. **8** Turf-cutter for digging ramparts. **9** Bronze mess-tin. **10** Netted bag, perhaps for rations; from three to fifteen days' food was carried.

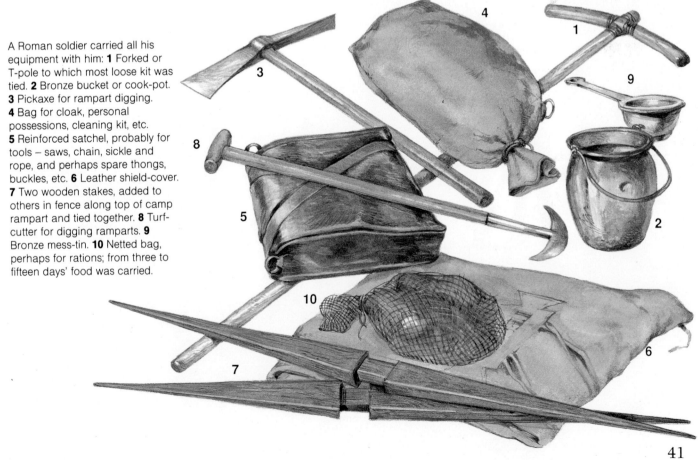

3

Soldiers at Isca

A man in a scarlet cloak and plumed helmet rides up and dismounts from his horse. An orderly runs up to hold its bridle. The man nods approvingly at the gangs of working soldiers and wanders over to where we are standing.

'They are doing well, aren't they?' we say.

'Of course. And they don't need me to tell them what to do. You see, I'm the legate. I command the legion which will be stationed here – the Second Augustan Legion.'

'How many men will be based here?'

'There ought to be about 6,000 men in a legion but there are always men sick, on leave, or sent away for special duties – I'll be lucky to muster 5,300 of them.

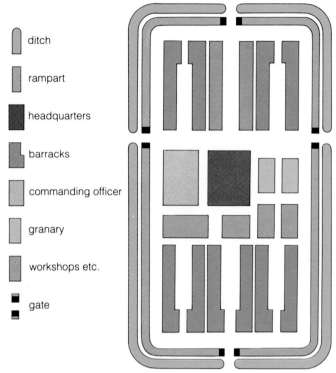

ditch

rampart

headquarters

barracks

commanding officer

granary

workshops etc.

gate

A plan of the fort at Isca

'A legion does more than fight battles – it lays out roads, builds bridges and, of course, forts like this one. Over there some of my men are helping to build the 'principium' – the command centre. That is where my office will be and where all my under officers and their clerks will work.

'As well as ordinary soldiers, I have all sorts of skilled workmen under my command. There are carpenters, blacksmiths, weapon makers, doctors, architects, surveyors, engineers and clerks. We call them "Immunes" because they're excused ordinary army duties. Such as sentry duty, which no one likes,' he adds with a smile.

'*It's all very impressive,*' we say.

'Yes, I suppose it is. Just Roman organis-ation and efficiency, that's all. When we've finished, we'll have quite a little town here, complete with barracks, workshops, parade ground, temples, baths, hospital, bank, corn stores and armoury as well as my house in the principium.'

'*How long will you be here?*'

'I don't really know. I hope one day to return to Rome and help run the empire and make its laws. I come from an upper-class family and no one but a man from my class can command a legion or be a member of the imperial senate in Rome itself.

'While here, I have junior officers to help me – five young tribunes, in fact, all hoping to be legates some day. But the key man won't be an upper-class officer at all. That's the camp prefect, a professional soldier who has risen through the ranks. He controls everything and everyone from the centurions down. From his title you'd think a centurion had a hundred men under him. He did once, I suppose, but now it's only eighty legionaries.

'*Why did you pick this particular place for your fort?*'

'It's near the sea so our supplies will be safe. We can control the river estuary. There's a river nearby for our water – for drinking, bathing, cooking, et cetera. We aren't far from other forts and the roads between them help us control the local Celts – the Silures, that is.'

'*What will the fort be called?*'

'Isca. I'm told it's just the Celtic word for water but the name's stuck – Isca of the Silures.'

He might have been amused to know that almost 2,000 years later, the site would still be known as 'Caerleon', or 'Fort of the legionaries'!

An aerial view of Caerleon today, with the fort in the foreground

Isca After Many Years

A hundred and forty years later the fort had been almost completely rebuilt in stone. The gateways are of stone with courses, or bands, of bricks at different levels. The houses of the legate and tribunes are near that of the camp prefect at the centre or 'principium'. The barrack blocks stretch out in rows where the tents once stood, although some look deserted and in need of repair. Some soldiers seem to be dismantling the bath building. What is happening?

What remains of the fort's baths today

There doesn't seem to be anyone around to ask. Even the amphitheatre is empty. We look around the oval tiers of seats – stone at ground level, wooden above. It's no use asking any of the working party – they won't know anything. Let's look at the 'vicus', the area outside the walls where the civilians live. Some are shopkeepers or traders, others are retired soldiers. Some are even serving soldiers who've married local girls – even though it's against military law: legionaries mustn't marry until they have served their time with the eagles.

Ah! Now there's someone we know. It's Tadia Exuperata, the daughter of a prosperous ex-soldier. The family live here but it's the first time she's been shopping in the vicus since the news came that her brother had been killed whilst serving with the eagles in Germany. She

is greeted by another shopper – the camp prefect, Publius Sallienus Thalamus.

'I was sorry to hear about your brother,' he says.

'It's been a difficult time, Publius. He had so much to live for.'

'But he died like a true Roman.'

After a few minutes, we tactfully break into the conversation and ask the prefect why the baths are being dismantled.

'We have orders to move the soldiers north to help protect the northern frontiers against the Picts and Scots.'

'*You mean that the soldiers are moving out of Isca Silurum?*'

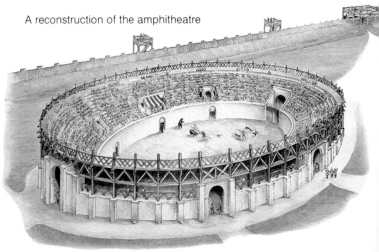

A reconstruction of the amphitheatre

Isca's barracks in the snow

Aerial view of the amphitheatre today

Publius smiles. 'They think they are,' he says, 'but I'm working very slowly and only sending men and materials up north in very small units. If we hang about long enough, I'm sure we'll get orders to put everything back again. We won't leave Isca if I have anything to do with it!'

Tadia says, 'It's been a worrying time here for years now. The empire has seen civil war, rival emperors, rising prices and huge increases in taxes. There would be serious trouble here if the soldiers left.'

'Well, we're all in it together,' says Publius. 'We're all Roman citizens now, aren't we? Not like the old days when you had to be born in Rome to have any rights. Or at least to have served in the army for twenty or twenty-five years.'

'That's right, Publius,' says Tadia, 'and the new emperor has been good to you soldiers. You are better paid than you've ever been.'

'Yes,' agrees the prefect, 'and we'll get some of our pay in food and goods.'

'The tribes may not like that part,' says Tadia. 'After all, they will have to provide the food.'

'That's true,' nods Publius, 'but the tribal chiefs live so much like Romans themselves now that they'll probably put up with it.' Another thought strikes him as he prepares to move away. 'Don't forget that there are now thousands of native-born Britons serving abroad as legionaries. Won't they do just as well out of the new system?' He laughs as he waves us goodbye, and heads back towards the fort.

Gold coins found at Isca

Gold for Rome

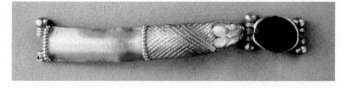
This bracelet was made with Dolaucothi gold.

The Romans made the most of all that Britain had to offer. Farm produce fed the garrison troops. Salt was mined in Cheshire. Lead came from the lands of the Deceangli in Clwyd and from the Cardigan area. They got tin from Cornish mines, copper from Anglesey and silver from North and West Wales. But the most valuable metal the Romans took was Welsh gold.

The Welsh gold-mine that the Romans dug can still be seen today. It is in a quiet, country district of Dolaucothi, where fast rivers wind their way through green valleys from steep ridges to the north. Near the joining of the

away at the cave walls. We even lit fires against the rock and then poured buckets of water over it to get it to crack and break. After that we made tunnels into the rock, to follow the vein of gold we found.'

'*Who looked after the slaves?*' we ask.

'Ordinary soldiers to start with but they were quickly replaced by Asturians from Spain. Asturians come from a gold-mining area and are experts at this sort of thing. They do the planning, the main engineering work, and look after the water supply.'

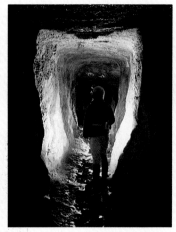

One of the adits (horizontal entrances) to the Roman mineworkings and (*right*) the interior of the main adit

The end chamber. Marks made by Roman miners' adzes can still be seen today

rivers Twrch and Cothi there is a place which has been called 'Ogofau' (caves). Here the Roman army began to dig for gold in the hills. They probably heard that there was gold here from prisoners or from their supporters among the Britons.

Let's go back to a time when the mine was working and ask a soldier to show us around.

'This is the place where the first work was done,' he says. 'We heard rumours that there was gold here so we brought in slaves to hack

Conditions were very cramped in the upper levels

46

'*You still crack the rock with fire and water?*'

'Yes. In some places we have too much water. The mines often flood. Come through here.'

As we go down one of the rock tunnels we can hear a rhythmic splashing noise. In the gloom we can just make out a gigantic wooden water wheel worked by slaves on a treadmill. Other slaves are helping the wheel to turn by pushing on the spokes. Around the outside of the wheel are buckets dipping into the flood water at the bottom and raising it to the top where it is emptied into a sluice which carries it away. Only a couple of lamps cast a feeble light in this cold and gloomy cavern.

Huge waterwheels were used to raise water from the mine

'Down here we have too much water. Above ground there is not enough. We need a constant flow of water to wash away the soil and gravel from the tiny particles of gold we find. We've made aqueducts – you know, water channels – from the river. One of them is more than seven miles long. We can direct the flow wherever we want. Some of it even goes to the pit-head baths.

'It's not much of a life for the slaves here but we don't believe in treating them too harshly. In fact the slaves have decent sleeping quarters and a canteen of their own. One or two of them even have fairly pleasant specialist jobs. You

see, we don't send all our gold straight off to Lyon or Trier to be minted into coins. No, indeed. A little of it stays here for a while and some of our skilled slaves fashion it into jewellery.'

'*Do you like working here?*' we ask.

The overseer pauses in thought for a moment, then he says, 'It's a pretty little spot but there's nowhere for the off-duty men to go. There's no town, no wine shop or anything like that. Fortunately, they don't have to stay here for more than a few months.'

'*The slaves do,*' we say.

Two smaller entries into the workings – probably for ventilation.

The 'coffin' level – the tunnel was wider at the top to allow for the yokes of the slaves carrying ore out from underground – and (*right*) a Roman mortar used to crush the gold-bearing ore

In spite of the years of hard work at Dolaucothi only a very small amount of gold was mined during the Roman occupation of Wales. If the Romans had not had slaves who were forced to work for nothing but their food, they would probably never have bothered to try to mine gold at Dolaucothi.

Caerwent: a Town and its People I

In any town today, what are the things you see and hear? Among them will be crowds of people, shops, cars, lorries, pavements, goods for sale and people working. Many of these things could have been seen and heard in a Roman town, two thousand years ago. Which ones would you NOT have come across in a Roman town? Cars and lorries, of course, would not have roared down the streets of a Roman town like Caerwent, a few miles from Caerleon. But there would have been traffic – horses and mules carrying goods, and heavy carts trundling down the muddy roads. It would have been just as silly to stand in the middle of the road in Caerwent as it would be in Cardiff, Wrexham, Bangor or Carmarthen today.

Caerwent was probably first built as a small fort around AD 75–80 to control the tribe of the Silures. Some coins from that period have been found in the ruins. When the Emperor Hadrian came to Britain, he withdrew the soldiers from Caerwent and made it into a proper town.

We're going to Caerwent to have a meal with a man called Julius Paulinus. He meets us with his personal slave at the town gate.

'Have you been here before?' he wants to know.

We give a shake of the head. '*Never,*' we say.

'In that case, we could see something of the town as we make our way home.'

We go through the gateway and Julius tells us, 'Our town, Venta Silurum, was built as a small fortress about a century and a quarter ago. The Emperor Hadrian came here about eighty years ago and took the soldiers away. There was no need for them by then. As a result, the civilians who lived here at that time had to form the first town council, or "ordo" – someone had to collect the taxes, mend the roads, check weights and measures in the market, punish criminals and many other things.'

As Julius says the word 'criminals' we are walking past something scribbled on a wall. Julius glances at it as we go by but we can't read it. Someone else has tried to scratch it out. Either the scratcher-out or someone else has printed alongside the graffiti the word 'puniamini' which means 'shame on you!' Julius hurries us away.

'After the legions left,' he says, 'we had to help pay for walls to be put up all the way round. You'll have noticed that the two main gates are not quite opposite each other as they ought to be. I'm not quite sure why. Maybe the first buildings were not quite in line either. Venta has its buildings laid out in blocks called "insulae" with the roads running between them. Like most Roman towns, the plan is a grid or checkerboard one. I say "Like most Roman towns", but that doesn't include Rome itself, of course.'

'*That's right,*' we say, '*Rome isn't exactly a regular pattern of streets, is it? There are far more high-rise buildings in the capital, such as blocks of flats eight or ten storeys high, because of lack of space and the high cost of building sites. Venta looks more like a Roman provincial or country town – Herculaneum, perhaps.*'

Julius ushers us into his house and leads the way through the entrance hall, or atrium, to the dining room, or triclinium. At dinner, each guest will lie full length on a kind of couch, supporting his head on one hand and feeding himself with the other.

Most of the main rooms are paved with mosaic tiles and the walls are painted with landscapes or pictures of gods and heroes. In the very centre of the house is a small formal garden, surrounded by covered corridors with rooms leading off them. There is a water supply but rain is also collected from the roofs and garden and stored in containers, to flush the toilets.

This house, like many others belonging to the wealthy, has hypocausts. This means that the space below the floor is hollow. Slaves light furnaces just outside the building and the hot air circulates under the concrete floor to keep people warm in the winter.

The meal starts at about eight o'clock in the evening and goes on till midnight or beyond, after which slaves will escort us to the inn where we are staying the night.

A silver coin showing Emperor Hadrian

A reconstruction of a dining room in a Romano–British house

Caerwent: a Town and its People II

Next day we find ourselves talking to the owner of the inn where we have been staying. The owner is a woman, Cornelia Sevenus. She tells us a little more about the town.

'My family,' she says, 'has lived here in Venta for generations. My father was once an important member of the ordo. Those were good days. Now, sadly, I'm the last of the family. All my other relatives are dead. I'm a Roman citizen, it's true, but I'm also a Silurian. My ancestors were warriors who ruled all the land around here. From the mountains and the valleys down to the rich lowlands along the coast, as far as the great forest of Dena, our people were masters until the legions came.

'Oh, I suppose most of us have become Romans – even our names are not what they would have been without the Roman occupation – but although we've changed our way of life, we haven't forgotten the past. In our temples we still make offerings to our own gods, and out in the country, the people still live much as they used to do.

'We had our own forts on the hills once, where the chiefs met. They were proud to serve under Caradog, fighting the legions, although he wasn't of our tribe. I suppose that, as a Roman, I should give the man's Roman name, but there's a lot of Celt left in me!

'The Romans built the great fort at Isca to control us and then they turned this little fort at Venta into a town for our leaders. This is the "civitas" – the centre for running the affairs of the whole tribe of the Silures. They took land hereabouts and gave it in small amounts to newly retired soldiers, hoping that mixing with centurions and men like that would make us all Roman a little more quickly.

'Our new rulers were not warriors or noblemen like our own people – they took more land from us and raised the taxes higher and higher to pay for the work of the army. Our farmers found that they'd either have to give more and more of their produce to supply the army or pay a bribe to some Roman official. In some cases, there wasn't a lot of difference between these choices. No wonder there were rebellions!

A marble bust of Emperor Hadrian

'Still, by the Emperor Hadrian's time things were quieter. He came here, to Silurian territory, and ordered the legion that was at Isca to go north. They were up there for years building a great wall to keep out the Picts.

'We lead a much more settled life in Venta now. I think you've been told how the town walls were rebuilt in stone – but there's very little danger here nowadays. We Britons own quite a lot of property in Venta. Many of our women have married soldiers from Isca or one of the other forts. Some have gone with their husbands to run farms after the men have retired from service. Others run shops and businesses in the town.

'Do you know that there's a very good seafood shop in the town now? My tribespeople were always good fishermen as well as farmers. I'm told that fish is very expensive in Rome. Is that right? I've never been to Rome – never left this area, in fact. I own this inn, which my husband left me when he died. That's one thing I'll say for the Romans – their law at least lets a woman inherit and own property. At least it does now, although I'm told it wasn't always so.'

Work in progress on Hadrian's wall

4

A Roman Villa Mystery

Roman bowl and flagon

There were many Roman country houses, or villas, scattered about the settled areas of Britain. Many have been found along the eastern side of the River Severn. There were comparatively few in what is modern Wales and those that have been found are mostly in the south and around fortress towns such as Deva (Chester) and Viroconium (Wroxeter).

A villa might be a single block building with a pitched roof, or it might be a large quadrangle of buildings enclosing a garden. The picture shows what it might have looked like shortly after it was first built.

Villas were really manor houses, at the centres of vast estates. Most villa owners made their money by farming or by leasing farms.

Some relied on other local industries such as wool production, weaving, pottery, or tile and brick making, to bring in the profits.

At Llantwit Major, a small town in South Glamorgan, the remains of a Roman villa have been discovered. When John Storrie first started to excavate the site in 1888, he found that the villa had been a large house with underfloor heating and its own bath-house.

Reconstruction of a Roman Villa. **1** main reception room, **2** living room, **3** bedroom, **4** cold bath, **5** hot room heated from below by the hypocaust, and **6** lavatory

Some rooms had mosaic floors and plastered walls covered with painted pictures. Lots of broken glass pointed to the use of glazed windows. Traces of lead and iron making were found in one of the work-shops around the courtyard.

Archaeologists have discovered that the villa was built about AD 150 and was lived in for at least a century and a half. Its owner must have had plenty of money, made perhaps from farming or from trade along the nearby coast – or even from a mixture of the two.

As John Storrie continued to dig he discovered a sinister secret that had been kept for centuries. In the various rooms of the villa, he and his helpers found skeletons: skeletons of three horses and no fewer than forty-three people. Storrie's report on the dig says that the skeletons were '... in all sorts of positions on the floor, some on their faces, some on their backs, some stretched out, some crouched up...'.

What could have happened? We know that the century after AD 300 was a violent and dangerous time in Britain. Rival Roman generals fought each other for the imperial throne. As Roman armies destroyed each other, invaders called 'barbarians' began to threaten the boundaries of the empire. As well as invaders searching for somewhere to settle, there were boatloads of bloodthirsty pirates looking for loot and ready to kill anyone who tried to stop them.

Sometimes the owners of villas, if they were frightened enough, would bury their money

Examples of fine Roman pottery called Samianware

and valuables, hoping to dig them up when the danger was over. Hoards of this type have been discovered in modern times, but nothing like it was found at Llantwit Major. Of course, if valuables had been buried and robbers found them, there would be nothing left for modern archaeologists to unearth.

We shall never know the true story of the last days of the villa. Perhaps the end was too sudden for any preparations or defence to be made. Perhaps there was a terrible massacre by pirates, leaving the villa ransacked and littered with corpses. John Storrie was sure that the bodies had not been carefully or deliberately buried.

A reconstruction of a Romano–British kitchen

Eventually, all the bones were removed and the rooms cleared out. Any clues from which modern archaeologists might have solved the mystery were lost for ever.

In the 1930s, in a different part of the same site, diggers found some more skeletons. These had apparently been laid out decently and buried properly, even though the burial had taken place after the villa was in ruins.

So, did a band of barbarian raiders come in with the tide one dark night while the family and slaves were fast asleep in their villa? Was the villa allowed to crumble away only to be used as a cemetery by local people many years later? What of the horses among the human skeletons? We shall probably never be sure. What do you think happened?

4

Roman Twilight

For almost four hundred years there were strong Roman armies in Wales and England. Can you imagine how long a time that is? If you count back from today it takes us back to the years when William Morgan was translating the Bible into Welsh.

The Romans never conquered Ireland. They believed that the Irish would never be brave enough to cross the seas and attack their strong forts in Wales. But the Romans did take armies into what we now call Scotland. They soon decided that the land was of no use to them. They built a wall and a chain of forts to keep the Picts out of England.

For three hundred years the Romans kept Wales and England safe from their enemies. In these peaceful times the Celtic peoples of Wales grew quite prosperous. They farmed the land, fished the seas, and sold their goods to the army and in the new towns the Romans were building. In many ways the Britons of Wales became like the Romans.

Their leaders lived in Roman towns or in villas built to Roman plans. They were protected by Roman laws and learned the Latin language. Welsh Britons fought as auxiliary soldiers in the Roman army. In some ways the Romans who settled in Wales became like the

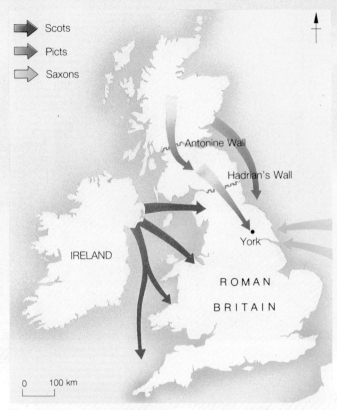

The direction of raids by Scots, Picts and Saxons on Roman Britain.
Note that the Scots did not originally come from the area we now
call Scotland

Britons. They worshipped the old Celtic gods
together and married Celtic women. In other
ways they stayed Roman. Their real loyalty
was to the Roman Empire and the city of Rome,
and not to the land they had settled in.

During the last hundred years of Roman
occupation, there were problems. Perhaps the
soldiers grew lazy and over-confident. Perhaps
the Roman Empire was too big to manage
properly. Eventually all the borders of the
Roman Empire were attacked by barbarian
tribes. Scottish tribes and the peoples of the
Scandinavian countries began to raid England,
and Wales was attacked by the Irish. But
instead of fighting the barbarians, the Roman
legions began to fight each other for control of
the empire. More and more soldiers were re-
called from Wales and England to fight Rome's
wars in Europe. By the year AD 410 the last
Roman troops left the British Isles. The Britons
were told that from now on they would have to
look after themselves.

4

Macsen Wledig – the Dream

Caernarfon Castle today

Seven hundred years ago, a great castle was built by the King of England, Edward I, at Caernarfon. At about the same time a story was written down in Wales about a Roman emperor called Macsen, who was supposed to have lived nine hundred years earlier at a time when the Romans still ruled Wales. In the story, Macsen is out hunting. He sits down, falls asleep and has a dream.

'He saw a great city at the mouth of the river, and in this city a great castle, and he saw many great towers of various colours on the castle. Inside the castle he saw a fair hall and two auburn haired youths playing at chess. The garments of the youths were of pure brocaded silk, and frontlets of red gold held their hair in place.... And he saw a maiden sitting before him in a chair of red gold.... And the maiden arose to meet him from the chair of gold, and he threw his arms around the maiden's neck, and they both sat down in the chair of gold.'

The story goes on to tell how the emperor falls in love with the girl in his dream and orders his soldiers to search for her. After three years of searching, Macsen himself comes to Aber-seint in North Wales. There he finds the beautiful princess named Elen. They marry

56

and have two sons whom they name Constantine and Publicus. Maxen gives three great castles, at Caernarfon, Carmarthen and Caerleon to Elen, and orders that fine straight roads be built between them.

The sites of Roman forts in and near Wales

Do you think the story of Maxen's dream is true? Let's look at the evidence. Remember it was not written down, as far as we know, until nine hundred years after Maxen's death, but it was likely that it had been told for many years before this. If you walk around Caernarfon you will find place-names that are linked with Roman times. There is a very old street named Constantine's Road, a parish church named after Saint Peblig – which sounds like the Roman name Publicus – and across the river there is a woodland park called Coed Helen.

Llanpeblig Church in Caernarfon

Could this mean that Maxen, Elen and their two sons did once live in Caernarfon? Or could these names have been chosen by people in the Middle Ages who had heard about Maxen's dream?

Macsen Wledig – the Evidence

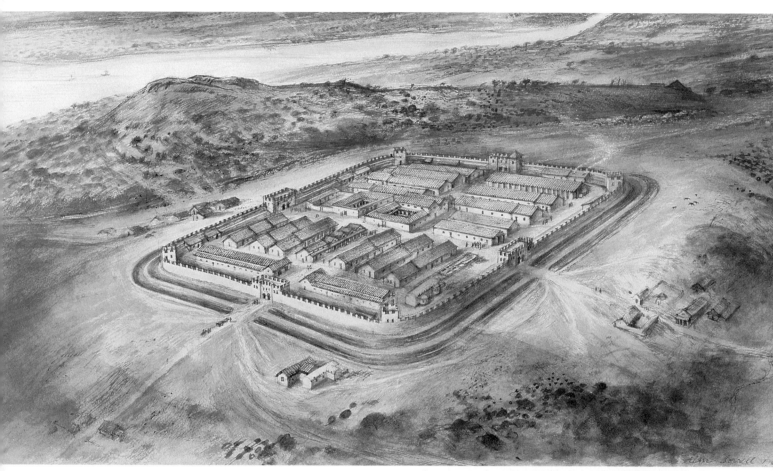

A reconstruction of the Roman fort of Segontium

There is certainly evidence that there were once Romans living in Caernarfon. We know there was a large Roman fort called Segontium at the mouth of the River Seiont. We also know, from old writings, that there was a Roman general called Magnus Maximus. He was probably born in what is now Spain. He came to Britain in AD 369 and won a great victory over the Picts some years later.

Fourteen years later his soldiers decided he should be emperor, and he left Britain to fight in Gaul. He set up his capital in Germany, and ruled there for five years before being defeated and killed in battle in AD 388. There are coins in existence with his head on them.

Coins showing the general Magnus Maximus

But none of the Roman writers mentioned his wife Elen, nor is there a word about Wales and Caernarfon.

Was Magnus Maximus the same person as the man in the Welsh legend? If he was, did he really marry a Welsh princess? A monk called Ambrosius who lived at the same time as Magnus Maximus wrote a story of his life in which he says he only had one son, whose name was Victor.

What about the evidence in favour of the legend? A stone pillar which stands near Llangollen mentions Macsen and says that a Welsh king called Cyngen of Powys, who lived in the Middle Ages, was descended from him.

There is another interesting piece of evidence written by Gildas, a monk who lived one hundred and fifty years after Macsen's death. He blamed Macsen for taking his soldiers away from Britain to help him become emperor. They were supposed to be defending the island against invaders.

Gildas does not mention any links with Caernarfon, but there is one other small piece of evidence. We know from an old Roman list that soldiers from Segontium were fighting in what is now Yugoslavia some years after Magnus Maximus's time.

The Pillar of Eliseg, a Roman pillar found near Llangollen

The site of the Roman fort of Segontium seen in an aerial view of Caernarfon

Cunedda and the Irish

Part of a Welsh alphabet chart from 1900 showing the Ogham alphabet

THE BETHLUISNION. (OGHAM ALPHABET)

Most of the Roman troops left Britain in the thirty years or so after Magnus Maximus's time. This meant that there weren't many soldiers left to protect the country from invaders or enemies. At once the Irish saw their chance. They began to pour across the Irish Sea, landing along the south-west coast in particular and then travelling further and further inland along the sturdy Roman roads. Some of these tribes may have been thrown out of Ireland, others had to flee because of problems at home and others may have come to Wales in search of slaves.

These raiders and settlers have left memorials in Wales which we can see today. They are large stones, erected in memory of well-known leaders during the fifth and sixth centuries. We know that they are Irish because the writing on the stones is in the ogham alphabet, and there are similar stones in Ireland today. The ogham alphabet has twenty letters based upon a special pattern of straight lines. About 40 ogham stones have been found in Wales, some in north Wales but most of them in the south-west in the Dyfed area.

It is obvious that during these centuries the Irish were a very serious threat to the way of life of the people in Wales. What could they do to protect their land? Who would come to lead them in battle against the invaders? The answer to their problems was found in a man named Cunedda Wledig or Cunedda the Emperor. According to the story, he was invited, perhaps by a Roman general, to come down from the Kingdom of Manaw Gododdin in the south of Scotland to get rid of the Irish from north Wales. So he came and settled in Anglesey. He began to fight the Irish with such 'immense slaughter' that they were driven out and they never returned to north Wales, to the area between the River Dee and the River Teifi.

In this important task Cunedda was helped by his eight sons and one grandson, and to thank them for their help he divided the land that had been conquered between them. The areas these sons settled in were named after their new conquerors and protectors. Ceredig (Cunedda's son) gave his name to the area called Ceredigion in Dyfed, Edern (another son) gave his name to Edeyrnion near Corwen in Clwyd and Meirion (Cunedda's grandson) gave his name to Meirionnydd in Gwynedd. We can imagine this great family and all their warriors travelling down from the Old North (south-west Scotland) and settling as Christian kings in this part of Wales. All the later kings and princes in north Wales liked to claim that they were descended from this particular family because it made them feel important in the history of Wales.

This story about Cunedda's great success is recorded for us in a book written in Latin and called the *History of the Britons*. The author was a historian called Nennius who lived in about AD 800, some four hundred years after Cunedda's journey south. Can we be sure that this history is correct? Are there any parts of the story which make you feel suspicious about it? Is the pattern of naming areas after Cunedda's sons just a little too tidy and convenient to be true? These are some of the questions that have worried later historians about

An ogham stone in St Dogmael's Church, Dyfed

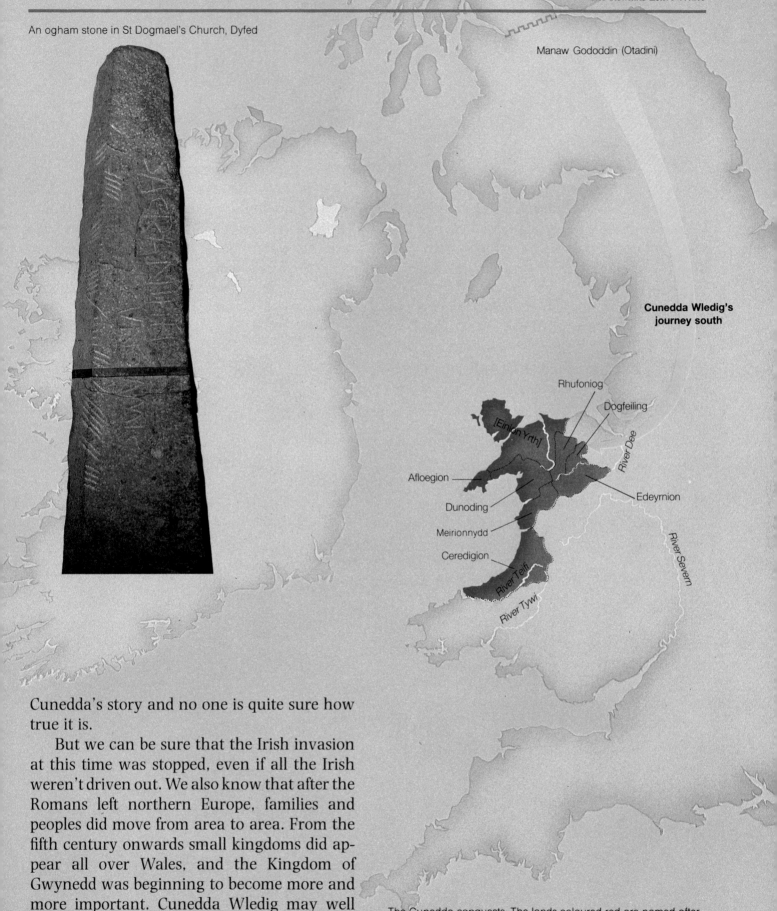

Manaw Gododdin (Otadini)

Cunedda Wledig's journey south

Rhufoniog

Dogfeiling

[Einion Yrth]

River Dee

Afloegion

Edeyrnion

Dunoding

Meirionnydd

River Severn

Ceredigion

River Teifi

River Tywi

Cunedda's story and no one is quite sure how true it is.

But we can be sure that the Irish invasion at this time was stopped, even if all the Irish weren't driven out. We also know that after the Romans left northern Europe, families and peoples did move from area to area. From the fifth century onwards small kingdoms did appear all over Wales, and the Kingdom of Gwynedd was beginning to become more and more important. Cunedda Wledig may well have played his part in this history after all.

The Cunedda conquests. The lands coloured red are named after Cunedda's sons and grandson

4

Arthur

You have probably heard of King Arthur of the Britons, the brilliant leader of the Knights of the Round Table. Children in France, Spain, Germany and England will have heard of him too, perhaps through the cartoon film 'The Sword in the Stone' or through reading the well-known legends about him.

One story tells how Arthur was badly wounded in the Battle of Camlan. Sir Bedivere, one of his knights, hurried over. Arthur said 'Take my sword Excalibur,' he said, 'and throw it into the lake.' Bedivere couldn't believe his ears! But he was faithful to his leader and he took Excalibur and walked towards the lake. He tried to throw away the magic sword, and tried again, but he could not bear to do so. Arthur was angry with Bedivere for disobeying orders and sent him to the lake for a third time. Bedivere ran towards the lake and, in tears, threw the lovely sword into the deep water.

Out of the lake came a white hand to catch the sword and draw it safely into the water.

When Bedivere returned to Arthur he found that he was becoming weaker and weaker. Arthur asked his faithful knight to carry him to the lake side. Suddenly they saw a beautiful boat sailing towards them. In it there were three young maidens dressed in black. 'What do they want, Lord?' asked Bedivere.

'They have come to take me to the Isle of Avalon', replied Arthur.

'But will I see you again?' asked Bedivere.

'I shall return', answered Arthur, 'when I am better – and when I'm needed.' With that, the boat floated away into the mist and Bedivere was left alone on the shore of the lake.

This is a strange and beautiful legend full of magic and mystery. Things like this couldn't really have happened, could they? There are no such things as magical swords like Excalibur and there is no such place as the Isle of Avalon. It isn't likely that there was anyone called Bedivere either or that there were Knights of the Round Table. These things all belong to the world of the imagination and fantasy, though the stories were so popular that people began to believe they were true.

Does this mean that Arthur himself never existed, and that his story is just another fairytale? What about the claim that he was Welsh – can this be true? We are not really sure. Even the books which were written around the time he was supposed to have lived make it difficult for us to decide. Gildas, the one writer who

Places connected with the legend of King Arthur

lived near to Arthur's time, in about AD 500, doesn't mention Arthur at all, even though he was supposed to have been such a super-hero. Perhaps Gildas had his own reasons for ignoring him.

Later writers, such as Nennius in his book called the *History of the Britons*, do mention Arthur. Nennius says that he fought many battles for the British against the Saxons, and that he wasn't a king at all but an important leader of a band of warriors, going from one place to another to help different kings fight against their enemies. He was so successful in the Battle of Badon (no one knows where this was fought) that the Saxons didn't attack the British again for over fifty years.

Before the fantastic stories about Arthur travelled to Europe and became known all over the world, his name was important in Wales and in Welsh writing. He is mentioned in poems and legends. One poem tells us that no one knows where Arthur is buried, and in the legend he disappears to the Isle of Avalon. He is one of the great heroes who are supposed to return to save the British or Welsh people when they call out for help. The Welsh always lived in hope that, one day, he would return to save and lead them.

Arthur's Stone, Cefn Bryn, West Glamorgan

63

4

Gildas

Gildas was born in 500 AD, the year in which the Britons won a great victory over the Saxon invaders. For many years after, the Britons enjoyed peace and security.

Gildas' family could remember the peaceful days of law and order when the Romans had ruled Wales. Gildas was taught to love Roman ways and the Latin language. He learnt about the heroes of Rome and the customs of its people. But, most of all he learnt about the stories and teachings of the scriptures. He had an excellent memory and could remember most of them by heart.

Gildas wanted to be a monk. At that time the most famous "school" for monks was at Llantwit Major in Glamorgan. The leading monk was a man called Illtud. He taught the young monks to follow a simple life, and trained them to become teachers and preachers. Many of these monks would spend their lives travelling around the country telling people about Christ and his teachings.

At the age of thirty-three, Gildas decided to write a book. It took him ten years to finish. Not everyone was pleased with what Gildas had to say.

Gildas said that the people of Britain had grown lazy and wicked during the years of peace. He warned people that God was angry with them; if they did not follow the teachings of Christ they would be punished with wars and plagues.

After writing his book, De Excidio Britanniæ, Gildas went around the country teaching and preaching. Although some people listened to him the majority took no notice. Gildas began to despair of making people change their ways. In the end he decided to leave Britain altogether and live in the part of France that is called Brittany. Here he continued his work until he died at the age of seventy.

You might think that once Gildas died people would forget about him. This was not so. Just as Gildas had warned, the plague returned and once again the Saxons attacked Britain. Many people remembered what Gildas had said. Monks began to make copies of his book and passed them on to other people. We know a great deal about how people lived and thought in these times because of the book Gildas wrote.

65

The Age of Saints

Do you live in a town or village which starts with the letters 'Llan'; Llanelli, Llandudno or Llangrannog perhaps? Can you pronounce, as all true Welsh people can, the long place-name with two 'llans' in it –

LlanfairPwllgwyngyllgogerwchwyrndrobwll-Llandysiliogo-go-goch?

There are, in fact, over 430 places in Wales starting with 'Llan'.

The word 'Llan' means a piece of land closed in by a wooden fence. Within this fence, originally, there would have been a church and a group of Christians living together. When did the pagan Celts become Christians, and how were these settlements called 'Llan' created?

We know that the Romans brought the Christian faith with them to the island of Britain. In Caerwent, the Roman town of the south east, a pewter plate was found with CHI-RHO, the secret Christian symbol, marked on it. But many of the people living inland might not have heard of this new Christian faith.

A pewter plate found in Caerwent had an early Christian symbol engraved on it. The symbol is formed from the first two letters – chi (χ) and rho (ρ) – of the Greek word for Christ.

It was probably in the sixth century, when many holy men began to work as missionaries, teaching and preaching throughout the country, that Christianity became popular. There were so many holy men that this was called 'The Age of Saints'. These saints dedicated their whole lives to serving God. They turned their backs on the fierce fighting amongst the warlords and went to live in remote and lonely places. They built small churches in which to worship and cells in which to live. Soon other holy men would want to join them and a cell would grow into a kind of monastery. In time, a group of holy men would move on to start another centre. The settlement or 'Llan' a saint started would be named after him. A story about the church of Llansadwrn will help to explain this.

About three hundred years ago a man was digging a grave in the churchyard at Llansadwrn. Suddenly his pickaxe struck a stone slab with strange markings on it. Although he probably couldn't read, he knew the markings weren't Welsh. He dug the slab out carefully and soon an expert arrived to examine it. The markings were in Latin, and although every letter wasn't clear, most of the words could be worked out. In English they read:

'HERE LIES BURIED BLESSED SATURNINUS
AND HIS SAINTLY WIFE
PEACE BE WITH YOU BOTH '.

If we look at the name on the stone and compare it closely with the name of the village:
SATURNINUS
LLANSADWRN
– we can see that they are very alike, and that the village was named after this Saint Saturninus or Sadwrn.

Although the saints worked hard to teach the people of Wales the Christian faith, they neglected the other parts of Britain, and under the Saxons and Angles England became more and more pagan. This is why, in the year 597, Pope Gregory I in Rome decided to send St Augustine to England, to convert the people to the Christian faith. Soon St Augustine realised that he should try to work with the Welsh saints and several meetings were arranged. The Welsh saints were worried about these meetings because they thought St Augustine might try to become head of all the churches in Britain. So, before they set out to meet him on the banks of the River Severn in south-west England, they asked the advice of a very wise holy man. His answer was: 'If St Augustine is a good man he will get up from his chair to greet you, but if he is a bad man he will remain seated.'

The Welsh saints travelled in their flimsy boat across the Severn to the English shore, where St Augustine sat waiting for them. Did he get up to greet them? No, he didn't. So the Welsh saints turned round and returned to Wales. They turned their backs on him and his church. The gap between the Celtic and Roman churches was not closed for many, many years.

Llansadwrn Church today, where the engraved stone shown below was found

The Age of Saints – How Do We Know?

How can we find out more about how the Welsh saints lived and worked? Their wooden churches and cells have almost all disappeared, or else later churches have been built on top of the old sites.

We could turn to the writings of a monk called Bede who finished his history of the Church of England in the year 731. But he was an Englishman and lived over a hundred years later than the Welsh saints, so it would have been difficult for him to know the whole truth.

Of course, there are all the stories in the books called the *Lives of the Saints*: the lives of Padarn, Dyfrig, Beuno and Cadog, who were important in their day. But these stories were written down so many hundreds of years after the saints had died that we can't depend on them too much, either.

There is one story, that of the life of St Samson, which is older than the rest. It was written down at about the beginning of the seventh century, fifty years after his death. The monk from Brittany who wrote it followed in Samson's footsteps and tried to gather as much information as possible about his life.

St Columbanus and St Gallus, two Irish pilgrim monks, crossing Lake Constance, Switzerland, while on their travels round Europe

Part of a 12th century manuscript showing St Samson, second from right

This 'Life of St Samson' tells us many things about the saints. In the first place it seems that Samson came from a wealthy family, and this was true of many of the other Welsh saints. They were men who chose not to become warriors or heroes because they wanted to serve God.

When he was five, Samson was placed in a monastic school at Llanilltud Fawr (or Llantwit Major) in the Vale of Glamorgan. Here he would have learnt to read and write; monks and priests were the only ones who learnt these skills at this time. The head of the school was St Illtud, a remarkably wise man according to the story:

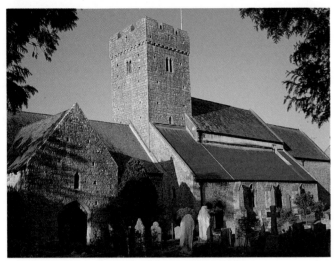

The church in Llanilltud Fawr (Llantwit Major) today

'The most learned of all the British in the Holy Scriptures, in the Old Testament and the New ... as well as in all branches of knowledge, such as geometry ... grammar, arithmetic and a knowledge of all the arts. He could also see into the future'.

It is not surprising that many of the Welsh saints came to Llanilltud Fawr especially to be taught by St Illtud. But after a while, St Samson began to feel that he wanted to live an even simpler life, so he moved to live amongst a group of saints on Caldy Island, off the coast of Dyfed. Even this simple life wasn't hard enough for Samson and he left Caldy to live in a cave on the sea-shore.

He believed that suffering would bring him closer to God, so he used to pray outside, naked, on winter nights. He refused to sleep in a bed. He preferred to lean against a wall all night to dream of God. One night he had a vision, or dream, which told him he should become a missionary, travelling far and wide to spread the Christian message.

At once he set out, wandering through Ireland and Cornwall before settling at Dol in Brittany and establishing a monastery there. This part of his life shows how far the early saints travelled, along Roman roads and in small boats on the open seas, to spread the Christian message. One historian has even claimed that they travelled 90 miles a day!

Whilst Samson was in Cornwall, according to one tradition, he saw a group of pagans worshipping an old stone pillar. He became very angry and began preaching to them about Christ. To turn their minds from the pagan gods he began to carve a cross in the stone. He might have explained this to his followers by saying: 'If you can't get them to change their old ways, then try to turn the old pagan customs into Christian ones'.

There are hundreds of Christian crosses or monuments from the Age of Saints in Wales today. Some are very simple, but others, like the beautiful tenth-century cross in Nevern churchyard, have intricately carved Celtic patterns.

It is hardly surprising that Cadw (which means 'to keep' in Welsh) has chosen the Celtic Christian cross as its emblem. Cadw is the organization which protects historic buildings and monuments in Wales. The Age of Saints left a lasting impression on Wales and the Welsh people.

The Cadw emblem

A Celtic cross from the Margam Stones' Museum

St David

This is a picture of Welsh people enjoying a slap-up meal on 1 March. St David's Day. Such scenes are familiar all over Wales.

Welsh people all over the world celebrate on 1 March. Children dress up in Welsh costumes and eisteddfodau, concerts and dinners are held to remind the Welsh people that this is the feast day of their own patron saint, Dewi, or David.

School eisteddfod on St. David's Day

Who was this St David? Why is he so important in the history of Wales? These questions should be easy to answer, because we have his story in a 'Life of St David'. We can read all about him. The story tells us that St David was remarkable even as a baby. When he was being baptized a well of sparkling water suddenly appeared. Later, he was sent to the school of the famous blind teacher, Paulinus. St David placed his hand over Paulinus' face and at once his sight was restored. David even managed to bring the son of a poor widow back to life.

Unfortunately, as we have seen, we cannot depend too much on this 'Life of St David'. It was written over 500 years after St David lived. The author, Rhygyfarch, a monk from mid-Wales, can't possibly have known what really happened in St David's time. Does this mean that nothing in the story is true?

Luckily, the answer is no. Rhygyfarch must have heard many stories about St David that had been passed down from father to son over the years. Parts of these stories were true. David was probably one of the early Welsh saints who travelled from place to place establishing churches as they went. Dewi or David can be found in many place-names especially in south Wales, from Llanddewi in Gwent to St Davids itself on the far coast of Dyfed.

Dewi's name is also found in Llanddewi-brefi, where, according to the story, a great crowd gathered to discuss religious matters. There were so many people that none of the speeches could be heard clearly. In despair, they asked St David to speak to them. He began to preach and his voice was like a loud trumpet. Suddenly the ground rose and lifted him up, so that everyone could see as well as hear him. Because of this great success, St David was considered to be the chief of all the Welsh saints. We don't have to believe this story, but we can be fairly certain that St David did visit the area and that an important meeting was held there. A stone has been found in the church wall at Llanddewibrefi with the words SANCTI DAVID carved on it.

We can also be fairly certain that St David lived a simple life. He was known as David the Waterman because, according to his life-story, he drank only pure water. There might be another explanation for this name. He might have been a member of a strange religious group who liked to punish their bodies by standing up to their necks in cold water every night. How would simple David the Waterman feel if he knew that St David's Day is celebrated by drinking and feasting today?

It is almost certain that St David died on 1 March in the year 589. According to his life story, before he died he greeted his fellow saints with these beautiful words: 'Brothers and Sisters, be full of joy and hold fast to your faith and belief, and do the little things you heard and saw from me.'

Although we can never be sure that St David said these words, they and the pattern of his life have touched the hearts of Welsh people for centuries. It is not surprising that Dewi Sant was chosen as the patron saint of Wales.

Modern statue of St David in Cardiff City Hall

The Welsh Language

A Welsh lesson in progress

The Welsh alphabet

Miss Williams has been giving the class a Welsh lesson. They've been learning how to describe the weather in Welsh.

'Mae hi'n braf' means 'It is fine' and *'Ydy hi'n boeth?'* means 'Is it hot?'

They've noticed that there isn't an 'it' in Welsh, everything is 'he' or 'she'. The weather is feminine so they say *'Mae hi'n braf'* which really means 'She is fine'. They've also noticed that certain letters change at the beginning of words. Hot is *'poeth'*, but it becomes *'boeth'* in *'Ydy hi'n boeth?'*. Miss Williams calls these changes mutations, but has told the class not to worry too much about them. She also says it's these points which make Welsh such a special language.

Glyn always enjoys the Welsh lessons, but there are a few things he doesn't understand. He decides to ask Miss Williams about them. 'Miss Williams, how old is the Welsh language?' he asks at last.

'That's a very difficult question to answer, Glyn', replies Miss Williams. 'Most people think Welsh developed as a language sometime during the fifth and sixth centuries. That's about 1,400 years ago.'

'In the time of heroes like Cunedda and Arthur,' chirps in Gwenno.

'And in the time of the saints, Samson and Dewi,' adds Glyn. 'But I still don't understand. What language was spoken here before Welsh developed, and why did it disappear?'

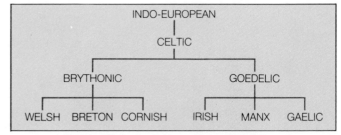

A family tree of the Welsh language

'It didn't really disappear, Glyn,' explains Miss Williams, 'it changed from the British language into a new Welsh language, just as British had developed many centuries before from the Celtic language. The British language must have been spoken all over Britain.'

'I thought lots of people spoke Latin – because the Romans were so important and strong,' says Gwenno.

'They did indeed, Gwenno, and the Latin language influenced the new Welsh language a great deal. The Romans gave us our alphabet and noblemen liked to have Latin on their memorial stones because it made them feel more important. The Welsh language borrowed over a thousand words from Latin.'

'Were these special words like "villa", "principia", and "civitas"?', asks Glyn.

'Some of them were, but even words for quite ordinary things were borrowed, like the word "murus", in Welsh "*mur*", which means a wall, and "fenestra" which is "*ffenestr*" in Welsh and means . . .'

'I know, a window,' answers Rhian.

'And, of course, the Romans brought religious words to do with Christianity. There's "*eglwys*" a church, "*llyfr*" a book and "*cannwyll*" a candle.'

Glyn had been thinking again. 'Did Welsh borrow words from any other languages – I was thinking of the Irish invaders and the ogham alphabet?'

'Very clever, Glyn,' answers Miss Williams. 'Yes, over the years Welsh, like every language, has borrowed lots and lots of words. Irish is Welsh's cousin because it is another Celtic language. The words for sandwich, "*brechdan*" and a cloth "*cadach*" are the same in both. There are probably many more words which are the same.'

'I still can't understand why this should have happened,' says Glyn.

Examples of Cornish words

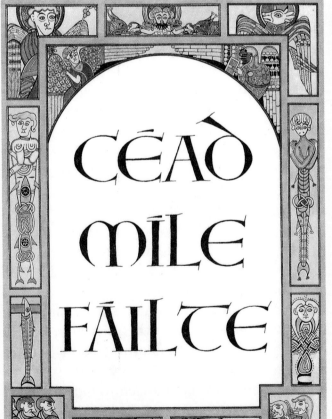

An example of Irish Gaelic

'Then you'll have to try and imagine what it must have been like to live in Britain in the sixth century. The Romans had left the island, the Saxons were invading from the east, the Irish from the west and the Picts from the north. The country was in chaos and confusion. People were learning new words and accents from each other. Out of this exciting jumble of sounds a new language, Welsh, came into being. It was born quickly in a rough and violent time. By about the year 600 it had become mature enough for poets to use it and, of course, it's still with us today. Now why don't we go back to learning about the weather in Welsh?'

5

Aneirin's Gododdin

It is an amazing fact that one of the first poems in the Welsh language does not come from Wales at all. It comes instead from the Old North, the south-west of Scotland, where the Welsh language was spoken in about AD 600.

The poem tells how three hundred noble warriors from the kingdom of Manaw Gododdin, under their fierce warlord Mynyddog the Wealthy, tried to stop the Angles and Saxons from conquering the whole of northern England. The warriors moved south and a bloody battle was fought between the Welsh and the English at Catraeth, or Catterick as it is called today. The raid was a disaster. Almost all of the Welsh were killed.

Imagine the desolation on the battlefield, with the bodies of the warriors and their horses and the crows circling above them. How sad the survivors would have been. What would Cynon the young warrior and Aneirin the poet do now? Let's eavesdrop on their conversation.

'I don't understand what went wrong with our attack,' says Cynon, 'after all, we spent a whole year at Mynyddog's court preparing for this raid. We discussed the plans in detail and ...'

'And feasted on his food, and drank his sweet, yellow mead,' continues Aneirin.

'Yes, but we have paid heavily for Mynyddog's mead. The dead have paid with their lives and have shown their loyalty to their warlord,' replies Cynon.

'They have. They were all so young, and yet in battle they were fierce and courageous,' remembers Aneirin.

'I shall never forget the sight of the long-maned stallions charging into battle, or the gleaming armour and the sound of the bright blue swords clashing,' adds Cynon.

'It was a sight to remember,' agrees Aneirin. 'It's not surprising that far more of the English were killed than the Welsh. There will be many sad mothers and wives crying for their lost menfolk today.'

'My heart is heavy, too,' sighs Cynon. 'A few days ago we were all laughing and joking together.'

'I look around the battlefield now and see all the faces I grew to know and love so well during our year of preparation,' says Aneirin. 'Noble Issac who came from the south to help us, Blaen who loved to wear clothes of gold and purple, and Rhufawn the Tall who was so generous with gifts to us bards. See, there are the bodies of Madog, Gwyn, Caradog, Owain ...'

'Don't name any more,' pleads Cynon, 'it makes me so sad. I think I'll go for another walk round the battlefield in case there is someone still alive. Don't sit there too long, thinking and grieving.'

Aneirin's mind was far away already. He would name his friends, all eighty of them, in a long, long poem. But it wouldn't be a sad poem. He would celebrate them as heroes – Welsh heroes. He was proud to be one of the first poets to write in Welsh, and the words were beginning to ring in his ears already. He would describe how they had drunk wine and mead from gold cups at Mynyddog's feast, and how they had rushed into battle full of joy. But he would also describe the deathly hush when the fighting stopped. The memory of these brave heroes should not be allowed to fade away. It was his, Aneirin's duty to make sure that did not happen. He would write one of the finest Welsh poems about them and he would call the poem 'Y Gododdin'.

A page from Aneirin's Gododdin

Cadwallon

'The news. Have you heard the good news?'

'Yes. That revenge has been taken and there's hope, a great deal of hope.'

News, revenge, hope. Those were the words on everyone's lips. The whole village bubbled with excitement like a cauldron of cawl, but no one seemed to be ready to tell Cadfan what it was all about.

All Cadfan could gather was that the news had something to do with Cadwallon, the King of Gwynedd, who had gone away with his men to fight a battle in the north. He also realised that no one would tell him more until the excitement died down, so there was only one thing for it, to go and look for Einion. Einion was the oldest man in the village and was also the wisest and cleverest man Cadfan knew. Einion always had plenty of time to chat, to answer questions and to explain matters.

Cadfan found Einion chewing on a blade of grass, and looking very seriously into the depths of the village pond. For a moment Cadfan thought that perhaps he had not heard the news.

'Einion, I wanted to ask you something,' he said.

'Well, Cadfan, you ask and I'll answer if I'm able.'

'Einion, what has happened? I know it's something to do with Cadwallon, and everyone in the village is very excited and shouting about revenge and hope.'

'Don't worry, my little man, I'll tell you. You see quite some time ago, before you were born, there was a very cruel Saxon king in Northumbria called Aethelfrith. He wanted to win our lands for himself and tried to do this by fighting his way south towards Chester. He was no Christian, but a pagan. When he got to

Can you see Cadwallon's name mentioned on this page from the Welsh *Chronicle of Kings*?

Chester, the Powys army was there to meet him. Many monks from Bangor Is-coed had gone there too, to pray for a Powys victory. Do you know what that pagan Aethelfrith did?'

'No,' whispered Cadfan; he knew from Einion's tone of voice that it would be something terrible.

'He killed twelve hundred of those good, Christian monks. Killed them stone dead.'

'That was terrible,' said Cadfan, 'monks don't fight.'

'Aethelfrith said that praying for victory was the same as fighting for it, that's why he killed the monks.'

'But what has that got to do with today's news?' asked Cadfan.

'At the time,' Einion carried on, 'we thought that we would be separated from our fellow Britons in Ystrad Clud as we had been from those in Cornwall and Devon. But Cadwallon has appeared as our leader, and today he has spilt the blood of the Saxon in revenge for the monks of Bangor Is-coed.'

'Has he killed Aethelfrith?' asked Cadfan, excitement sparkling in his eyes.

'Not exactly. You see, Aethelfrith died some time ago and Edwin, a Christian, is now the King of Northumbria.'

'I see, Cadwallon and Edwin are both Christians, so they are friends,' interrupted Cadfan.

'It's not quite as simple as that,' replied Einion. 'Edwin who is a very powerful king, forced Cadwallon to flee to Ireland. When Cadwallon dared to return, he made an agreement with Penda, the ruler of Mercia.'

'Is Penda a Christian as well?' asked Cadfan.

'No, Penda is a pagan,' answered Einion very quietly.

'I'm sorry Einion, but I don't understand. How can a Briton and a Saxon, let alone a Christian and a pagan, come to an agreement?'

'I don't really know. It's the first time its happened, and it seems to have worked,' puzzled Einion. 'Cadwallon's troops landed along the Northumbrian coast and marched inland, while Penda's troops attacked from the south. Edwin and his troops stood no chance and Edwin himself was killed.'

Bangor Is-coed today

'Oh!' cried Cadfan. 'We're safe. The agreement did work.'

'Yes,' agreed Einion, 'and the massacre of the monks has been revenged. Our men and Penda's killed, stole and burnt throughout Northumbria. The only thing I can't understand is how a Christian could steal gold and silver from monasteries, even Saxon ones.'

'Perhaps it was Penda's troops who did that,' Cadfan suggested.

'Maybe it was,' Einion agreed. 'Maybe we should forget about revenge and think of the hope.'

'What hope?'

'Until Edwin's death it looked as though the Saxons would conquer the Britons, but now there is more hope of the Britons, under Cadwallon, conquering the Saxons,' answered Einion.

Offa and Heledd

A coin showing Offa's head

If you have ever travelled along the M4 motorway over the Severn Bridge into Gwent in South Wales you will have noticed the sign saying 'Croeso i Gymru, Welcome to Wales'. Signs such as these are nowadays the only marks which show that you are crossing the border from England into Wales.

But about 1200 years ago, a very different kind of border was built between the two countries. It was a huge dyke or mound of earth, 128 kilometres long, which stretched from north to south Wales. Tons and tons of earth were shifted to create this dyke. In some parts it was over two metres high, and on the Welsh side there was a ditch two metres deep. On top of the mound was a wooden fence or stockade, although this has now disappeared. It seems likely that soldiers marched up and down along the dyke, guarding the border from enemies. In its time, the dyke must have been a formidable barrier between the two countries. Why was it built, and by whom?

During the second half of the eighth century the large and important Anglo-Saxon kingdom of Mercia in the centre of England was ruled by King Offa. He was a powerful leader and had already managed to conquer much of England. He had also led two raids into Wales, and he was becoming more and more tired of keeping watch over his troublesome neighbours. The people of Powys in particular were always raiding his kingdom, stealing his cattle and goods and snatching pieces of land. He decided it was time to build a border, an impressive dyke to show the Welsh which lands were his and which were theirs. Work began on Offa's Dyke.

To emphasise the difference between the people living on each side of the dyke, the Mercians called their neighbours Welsh, which means 'foreigners' in the Anglo-Saxon language. So the Welsh became foreigners in their own country! But the Welsh also found a name for themselves, a name that meant that those who lived west of the dyke were 'fellow countrymen', or 'Cymry'.

A view of Offa's Dyke today

Offa's new and impressive dyke brought an end to the fighting that had been going on for years between the kingdoms of Powys and Mercia. We know about these long-standing troubles through a series of beautiful Welsh poems. They describe the tragic deaths of the last kings of Powys, killed while defending their land against the Saxon enemies.

The story is told by Heledd, a royal princess of Powys. After the fighting she finds herself alone in the hall of her brother Cynddylan's court, at Pengwern near Shrewsbury. All the warriors – Elfan, Gwyn, Cynon and Cynddylan himself – have been killed. There is nothing left: no song, no fire, no candle nor bed in the hall tonight. All is dark, desolate and quiet – the hall and the kingdom have been laid waste by the enemy.

'Cynddylan's hall is dark tonight
    With no fire, no songs,
My cheek's worn out with tears.

It wounds me to see Cynddylan's hall
    With no roof, no fire
Dead is my lord, yet I live.'

Crying sadly, Heledd, dressed only in goats' skins and a thin cloak and leading only a single cow before her, wanders away from the hall to seek shelter in the hills. She has no reason to live now. Her family has been killed and her royal kingdom of Powys destroyed. She will weep for a little while, then she will be silent.

If you stand on Offa's Dyke today and look east towards the old kingdom of Mercia, then west towards the old kingdom of Powys, it is easy to see why Heledd, Princess of Powys, wept so bitterly. The country to the east is flat and fertile, while to the west the Welsh were forced to make do with the poorer, hilly land.

Vikings

An animal figurehead on the stern of a Viking ship

It was the cuckoo month and as was the custom of the Scandinavians, the young men of the village had left to go a-viking. Every year as soon as the spring ploughing and sowing was completed, the young men left their villages to trade with and raid countries far away over the seas.

Lief looked forward eagerly to the time when he could join the young men on their adventures. Next year he would be fourteen, his sea chest had been made and his education was nearly complete. From his father and the older boys he had learnt many things: how to handle weapons and to fight, and how to ride and swim. From the skald he had learnt the sixteen letters of the runic alphabet so that he could read. Yes, by now he could boast:

'There are nine skills known to me –
at the chessboard I am skilful,
Runic writing I know well,
Books I like, with tools I am handy,
Good with snow-shoes, rowing and shooting,
and expert with harp and verses.'

Lief wandered through the village feeling a little fed-up and restless. Yesterday had been a very good day. A pedlar had been to the village selling wonderful things which Astrid, Lief's mother, had bought with a weight of silver coins. The pedlar was a Swede. The Swedes traded in the countries to the east. Lief did not want to go trading to the east, he would prefer to go a-viking westwards and norsewards, probably because he was a Dane and that was the direction in which they went.

He remembered how much he had enjoyed the hunt the previous afternoon, when he and a few others had gone into the forests. Lief enjoyed the thrill of the hunt, especially if his horse was young and lively. Armed with a spear, longbow and arrows, they'd killed some red deer, a hare, a lynx, some woodcock and ducks. These would provide very tasty meals.

After the hunt, Lief had arrived home very hungry, and had been pleased to see that the meal was his favourite. It was a thick, rich stew made of meat, vegetables and left-overs, seasoned with salt, pepper, and other spices brought from the Eastern countries and sold to Astrid by the pedlar. It was all washed down with sweet honey mead. Later that evening, the skald had told them an exciting yet sad legend about Sigurd and Brynhild. Then Lief had snuggled under his eiderdown of soft goose feathers to sleep and dream of owning his own longship and going a-viking.

Lief strolled down to the sloping bank at the edge of the fjord where Kari, the village carpenter and Eirik, the village blacksmith were busily completing a new longship. Lief sat a little distance away and pretended that the ship was his.

It was to be a wonderful magical ship. Lief had watched and helped the young men do much of the early work before they had gone a-viking. He had helped when the great keel had been cut and shaped in the forest before being dragged by horses down to the beach. He had helped find pieces for the knees, ribs and crossbeams, and had watched the outside planking being prepared. The prow boasted an exciting pattern of strange animals, terrible enough to frighten any enemies.

The longship was about 17 metres long and had thirty oar-holes. Lief imagined himself at the steering oar, peering over the high waves and through the sea mist to the land. He would steer his ship into a secret creek from where he and the other Vikings would move inland to perform heroic deeds which the skald would relate on long winter evenings for years to come. He would bring back treasures and exciting stories.

All this he imagined as he watched Kari and Eirik at their work. Before he became too old he might be killed in battle. He could imagine his body being dressed in rich silk garments and placed on rugs beneath a tent on the deck of his ship. A beautiful young slave girl would be killed and laid at his feet. A great pile of wood beneath the ship would be set alight. The yellow and scarlet flames would reach to the sky and Odin's wind would carry his soul to Valhalla to hunt, feast and listen to wonderful legends for ever and ever.

How he enjoyed that day-dream. Still, it would not be long now. The next cuckoo month was on its way.

Routes of Viking raids on the British Isles

ATLANTIC OCEAN

VIKING HOMELANDS

North Sea

IRELAND

ENGLAND

WALES

Baltic Sea

0   500 km

5

Rhodri Mawr

When Rhodri Mawr became King of Gwynedd in 844, it was at a time when kings had to fight to keep their kingdoms and safeguard their subjects. Rhodri knew that his reign would not be peaceful, but he was determined that it would be a great one. He wanted to become king of all the other parts of Wales, as well as Gwynedd. If he could do this, Wales would be one strong country; strong enough to keep the Saxons on the other side of Offa's Dyke, and strong enough to keep the Vikings away.

The Vikings were constantly raiding, stealing, burning and killing along the coast of Britain. Wales was unlucky because it lay in the path of the Vikings, and the lands of Anglesey, Dyfed and the Severn Valley were fertile. There were also churches and monasteries in the sheltered areas around the coast, in places such as Holyhead, Penmon and St Davids. The Vikings enjoyed stealing the gold crosses and chalices from these churches and killing the beef cattle on the fertile land for meat. Trying to protect these places was dangerous and often ended in death.

Viking warriors carved in stone

An axehead made from iron and inlaid with silver, found in Denmark

One of the people who was killed was Cyngen. No one knows why he was killed by the Vikings. Perhaps he was trying to protect his possessions, or maybe he merely wanted to find out who these strangers in their longboats were. All we know is that his death is the first to be recorded in the *Brut y Tywysogion* (A history of the Welsh Princes). The entry reads like this:

'Eight hundred and fifty was the year of Christ when the pagans slew Cyngen.'

The Welsh entry tells us that he was found strangled:

'Ac y tagwyt kyngen y gan y kenhedloed.'

('And Cyngen was strangled by the invaders.')

This was the beginning of many cruel raids, on Anglesey in particular. It was the Danes from Ireland who began these raids. They were trying to get a foothold in Wales. Some succeeded by moving deeply into the country along the rivers Dee and Severn, and preparing the way for others to follow. But the Vikings were not going to get it all their own way. Rhodri Mawr was going to see to that.

In 855, a fleet of Danish warships, long and narrow with oars along the whole of their sides, sailed from Ireland towards Wales. They were heading purposefully towards Gwynedd. They were going to raid Wales again, and hopefully some of the warriors would be able to make their way into Powys. On board, their double-edged swords, axes, spears and shields were laid ready. They knew all the possible landing places and quiet beaches, and at nightfall they pulled their ships to rest on a shelving beach. Excitement and battle fever were gripping their stomachs. They loved this kind of dangerous adventure, and if they were killed it meant they could go to Valhalla to live happily forever with Odin. Quietly they laid the oars in the boats. Each man, dressed in his tunic of leather, put on his iron or leather helmet. They picked up their weapons.

The Vikings didn't know that they had been sighted and a message was on its way to Rhodri. Here was a chance to avenge all the cruel raids on Anglesey. Rhodri gathered a strong army of determined Welshmen and faced the Danes for battle outside the town which is now known as Llandudno. The Danes had carefully planned battle formations, and probably used one of these in their battle against Rhodri.

In spite of their formation, double-edged swords and axes, many Danes died in the battle. The Welsh under Rhodri Mawr were victorious and Horm, the Viking leader, was killed.

6 The Rulers of Wales

Hywel Dda

Look at this picture. In it you can see a beautiful mosaic pavement and stone walls surrounding six small gardens. This lovely memorial was built in the little market town of Whitland, Dyfed, to help the Welsh people remember Hywel Dda (the Good), King of Wales 942-950. Why did they choose to plant a garden to remember him by and why was he the only Welsh king to be called 'Good'?

There was nothing in Hywel's early life to suggest he would become so famous. As the son of Cadell he knew that one day, he would inherit his father's kingdom, Seisyllwg, but he also knew that he would have to share it with his brother Clydog. Hywel took his grandfather, Rhodri the Great who had conquered the whole of Wales, as his example. If Rhodri had succeeded, why couldn't he?

His first step, in 905, was a clever one. He married Elen, the Princess of Dyfed, and so became King of Dyfed. A few years later, after his father died, his brother Clydog was killed. This meant that Hywel was now King of Seisyllwg and Dyfed together, a kingdom which came to be called Deheubarth. The King of Gwynedd and Powys at this time was Idwal Foel but in 942 he was killed by the English. At once Hywel led his forces north, drove Idwal's two sons out of their kingdom and declared himself King of all Wales. His rise to power would hardly have earned him the title Hywel the Good, would it?

Hywel travelled widely outside Wales. He went to Rome to see the Pope and he seems to have visited the courts of the Kings of Wessex, the main Anglo-Saxon kingdom, several times.

Hywel Dda, King of Dyfed

A coin inscribed with the words
HOVAEL REX (Hywel King)

Hywel also saw some good things on his travels and copied them. He noticed that many countries minted their own coins, and he became the first Welsh king to produce coins with his title HOVAEL REX (Hywel King) on them. He also noticed that the Kings of Wessex were powerful because their kingdom was ruled by one law. As soon as he had become King of Wales he called together six lawyers from every area in Wales, at a place called Whitland, in Dyfed, to examine the laws of Wales carefully. They threw some of the old laws out, they changed some and some they kept. These new Welsh laws have been kept for us in copies written about 300 years after Hywel's time. They have played a very important part in the history of Wales.

Could this explain why he was called Hywel the Good, and why his memorial is a garden in Whitland? Remember that a garden is a rough piece of land until it is cultivated. Laws also help turn rough and wild people into a civilised nation.

Why did he go there? William of Malmesbury, a historian who wrote 200 years later, suggests the answer. He says that Athelstan of Wessex forced the rulers of the Welsh to meet him in the city of Hereford and submit. They were to pay him 20 pounds of gold, 300 pounds of silver, 25,000 oxen, and some hawks and hounds annually.

This is how Athelstan showed that he was the main king and had power over Hywel and the other Welsh kings. It is not surprising that some of the Welsh were unhappy about this. One bard, in a poem called 'Armes Prydein', called out to the Welsh to join forces with the Scots, the Irish and the Vikings to drive these evil Saxons back into the sea. His message was a bloodthirsty one:

'There will be heads split open without brains,
Women will be widowed, and horses riderless,
There will be terrible wailing
before the rush of warriors.'

Hywel ap Cadell appears to have ignored this call. Perhaps he had no choice.

A sundial in the memorial garden to Hywel Dda in Whitland, Dyfed

6

The Welsh Lord's Hall

The steward and the falconer from the Welsh Laws

Let's spend an evening in the hall of a Welsh king in Hywel Dda's time. We know what to expect because the Welsh laws give us a good description of a hall and court.

Imagine we are listening to a conversation between two members of the king's bodyguard during a feast at the hall. One is an experienced soldier, the other a young man. They stand against the wall in the lower part of the hall, gazing past the raging fire in the centre of the room towards the king's table. The room is dark and smoky.

'Who are those people sitting at the king's table? Why have they got chairs instead of benches like everyone else?'

'They're the special officers of the court. Fourteen of them have their own chairs in the hall. Do you know, the chairs have to be arranged in the same order, even when we move from one place to another?'

'I suppose the one next to the king is the most important person in the area we're in now.'

'That's right. He's the chancellor and the king always likes to chat to him to find out about the farming in the area.'

'Someone's getting up.'

'That's the priest. We'd better be quiet for a moment. He's going to bless the food before they begin to eat.' The priest gets up and says the Lord's Prayer.

'Do you know, the priest's a very clever fellow, he can even read and write. No wonder the king says that he's one of the officers who must never get drunk at a feast.'

'That must be quite a strain – look at all the drink there is on the tables.'

'Yes, I must admit these feasts can become quite rowdy. They like to enjoy themselves drinking the mead. That's why the women don't come to the feast, I suppose.'

'I'd noticed they weren't here. Where are they?'

'Oh, the women have a chamber of their own. They can even call on someone to sing to them, as long as it doesn't disturb the men in the hall.'

'Does anyone sing here then?'

'Of course, a top-class bard – the Pencerdd. He's one of the king's main servants. If anyone's awake later on he'll get up and sing one of his new poems to the king. He can make you feel really proud you're working for such a generous and strong king.'

'Who does all the work, preparing the food and drink?'

'The distain is in charge of all that. He's the steward and he's becoming more and more powerful. He looks after the loot from our raids too. Don't annoy him, whatever you do.'

'I think I recognize the man at the end. Isn't he the chamberlain?'

'Yes, you're beginning to learn. He looks after the king's bed or chamber. He gathers clean straw for it and spreads out the bedclothes.'

'I'm almost ready for bed now. I don't think I can take in much more tonight. There seem to be so many different officers, each with a different job.'

'There are, and I haven't even mentioned the chief falconer, the groom, the doctor, the justice, the blacksmith, . . .'

'Stop, I'm exhausted. What a complicated place a Welsh king's court is!'

6

The Laws of Hywel Dda

The date is 1 November in the year AD 980. It is some years since Hywel Dda died, but the Welsh laws which he helped to bring together are still being used every day in the Welsh law courts. In the area called Maenordeilo in Dyfed the judge and lawyers of the local court are hearing all kinds of cases. Let's go into the court quietly, to listen to some of the cases for today.

The first case has been tried and judged already. Bleddyn ap Cadwallon of Maenordeifi was accused of insulting Dafydd ab Ieuan of Catheiniog. Bleddyn had sold Dafydd a black cat for three pence. He had claimed that the cat was an excellent mouser, and that it had good eyes and ears and sharp claws.

When Dafydd got home he found that the cat was deaf in one ear and that it was hopeless at catching mice. He had felt very angry, and had come before the court to demand his three pence back. The lawyers, after looking up the case in their law books, found that this would be fair. No one was supposed to sell a cat that wasn't up to a particular standard.

But ss-sh! The second case is about to begin. Einion ap Rhys is the guilty person. His crime is stealing a loaf of barley bread from a bakehouse in Llandeilo. Einion could be put to death for stealing. He is saying something to defend himself:

'Sirs, please listen to my pitiful story. I am a poor widower with four young children. I cannot work because I am a cripple and we have no food to eat. I beg food from the farms and villages, but this week I haven't been very successful and we have almost starved. That is

The judge from the Welsh Laws

why I stole a loaf of barley bread from the bakehouse. Have mercy on me. Do not send me to the gallows. I was in despair when I stole the loaf. Twelve of my relatives will swear my story is true.'

Everyone in the court feels sad when they hear this wretched tale. What will the lawyers do? Can they accept Einion's story and save his life? Yes, they can; the law books say that if someone has been forced to beg for food for three days, he cannot be sentenced to death for stealing food to keep himself alive. Einion ap Rhys can leave the court a free man.

The last case for the day is a difficult one. Two men have been murdered in a fight during the October fair at Llandeilo. The murderer, Iorwerth ap Cynfyn, stands before the court. His head is bent and he looks down at the floor. The two murdered men were a local nobleman, Llywelyn ap Madog and his slave, Hugh. Surely the court will send this murderer to the gallows?

But the law books have a different punishment for murder. Iorwerth is told he must pay a sum of money called a *'galanas'* for Llywelyn's death. Since Llywelyn was a nobleman, he was worth 84 cows. Hugh was a slave, so had no *galanas* value. He was only worth one pound, the same as an animal. Llywelyn's family, who are in the court to hear the sentence, are pleased with this arrangement. At least the families of the murderer and the murdered won't fight and shed yet more blood.

The court closes its business for the day. The Welsh laws have helped the lawyers to sort out some difficult problems and to keep order in the country.

Characters from the Laws

89

Women in the Welsh Laws

Characters from the Laws

It is difficult to imagine what life must have been like for a woman in Hywel Dda's time. The beautiful tale of Branwen, daughter of Llŷr, from the famous collection of Welsh legends called the *Mabinogi*, will help us to understand.

In the story Matholwch, King of Ireland, sails to Wales to claim Branwen's hand in marriage. Her brother Bendigeidfran, a giant of a man, is delighted at the offer. A great feast is held to celebrate the joining together of Matholwch and Branwen, of Ireland and Wales.

Unfortunately they forget to invite Efnisien, Branwen's quarrelsome half-brother, to the feast. When he finds out, he is extremely angry. Let's join the court story-teller as he sits by the fire in the king's hall, to find out what Efnisien does next.

'And with that Efnisien went for Matholwch's horses and cut their lips to their teeth, and their ears from their heads and their tails from their rumps, and where he could catch hold of their eyelids he cut them to the bone.

'As you can imagine, Matholwch was deeply insulted by this terrible act and he decided to return home at once. Bendigeidfran immediately tried to pacify him by showering him with expensive gifts: a new horse for every horse destroyed, a silver rod and a gold plate as large as Matholwch's face. Peace was restored between them and eventually Matholwch and Branwen sailed to Ireland.

'Branwen was welcomed warmly to her new home. Soon she gave birth to a son, Gwern, and all seemed to go well for the young family. But gradually the story leaked out of how Matholwch had been so badly treated in Britain, and the Irish people were very angry.

Matholwch was forced to punish Branwen by banishing her to work in the palace kitchen and by asking the butcher to box her ears every morning. What a dreadful fate for a wealthy princess!

'But Branwen was not so easily defeated. She made friends with a starling and sent it back to Wales with a message to ask Bendigeidfran, her gigantic brother, to come at once to avenge this insult to his sister. He came and the two countries fought in a bloody battle. In the end Branwen returned to Wales and died on the bank of the river Alaw in Anglesey of a broken heart.'

Branwen daughter of Llŷr's legend is a very sad one, but it is much more than a fairy-tale from the Dark Ages. If we look at the Welsh laws, we can see that Branwen's story fits in with the picture they give of how women in Wales were treated at this time.

Branwen was not allowed to choose her husband. She was handed over to Matholwch by her brother. Perhaps he thought he was doing the right thing and that it was his duty.

The story tells us that when Efnisien insulted Matholwch, his brother Bendigeidfran paid a huge price for the insult. According to the Welsh laws the price for an insult to a woman was much less than for a man. She was considered to be worth only half the value of her brother, and a third of the value of her husband.

English and Welsh laws were different. An English woman could inherit land and be an heiress. A Welsh woman couldn't. Her job was to give birth to sons and heirs. If she separated from her husband after seven years of marriage, however, she could claim half his belongings. She could ask for a divorce if her husband had leprosy or just bad breath!

Welsh women were thought of as weaker and less important than men, at this time. This is why it is so difficult to find out more about the history of women in Wales.

A Nobleman's Homestead

Let's journey back almost a thousand years to discover what life was like in the Welsh countryside at this time.

You would notice at once that there were hardly any towns. The few that there were – such as Caernarfon, Swansea, Milford, or Newport – looked more like villages when compared with the much larger towns of York, Hereford and Gloucester in England.

Most people lived from the land, either working it themselves or renting it to others. It isn't surprising that the Welsh people watched nature very carefully. Their poets observed its every mood. They feared the hard winter with its 'angry wind' and 'woods stripped naked'; and they feared heavy stormy weather which filled the rivers and flooded the countryside. Such bad weather could bring disaster to a family or tribe which depended on the land.

Our journey will take us to visit a nobleman's homestead in the district of Arfon in Gwynedd. As we walk along the path towards the homestead a man, dressed in a grey woollen robe, comes towards us. Perhaps he can tell us something about the pattern of farming here.

'*Bore da*', we say in Welsh, '*you seem in a hurry.*'

'I am,' he replies. 'You haven't seen any pigs on your travels, have you? I drove them into the forest this morning to feed on the acorns and thorns, and when I closed my eyes for a moment they disappeared. It's hard work watching pigs all day. I should know, because that's all I do – watch pigs every day.'

'You must be the swineherd then. How many pigs do you look after?'

'Twelve at the moment. Pigs are very important animals on our farm. The lord and his family enjoy a good meal of pig's meat.'

'What about you, swineherd?' we ask. *'Do you get to see any bacon or pork on your dinner plate?'*

'Hardly!' he laughs. 'No, I'm only a slave on the homestead. I have to obey my lord at all times and maybe I'll have tripe when they kill the pigs in the autumn.'

'Are there still slaves in Wales today? Didn't they disappear with the Romans?'

'I wish they had. No indeed, slavery has become worse during the last years with the Viking raids. I was born a slave here in Arfon and a slave I shall remain. My lord owns me, just as he owns the pigs I look after.'

'Is there no way you can become a free man?'

'I've heard that some slaves in the south have been able to save up enough money to buy their freedom,' he answers, 'but on the little money I get for being a swineherd that isn't possible. Excuse me now, I've got to find my pigs. Good-day to you.'

The swineherd walks away and we make our way towards Iestyn ap Cadwgan's farmstead. On the way we pass several hives of bees. These produce the honey which is so important in a time when there is no sugar, not only to sweeten food, but also to make the drinks of poets and heroes – mead and bragget. Around the farmhouse door chickens scratch busily.

'Come in strangers, come in;' shouts a hearty voice from inside. 'Welcome to Arfon. You're just in time for dinner.'

'Thank you, Iestyn ap Cadwgan' we reply, *'we have heard of the warm hospitality of the people of Arfon.'*

Soon the dinner is laid out on the heavy oak table and Iestyn urges us to eat well.

There is plenty of food to choose from: perch and trout from the lakes; beef from the cattle on the estate; milk, cheese and butter from the farm's dairy; and wheaten bread, a luxury in this time. You might notice that there

A farmer from the Welsh Laws

aren't any vegetables. Very few people keep gardens, they are too busy working out in the fields.

'*A nourishing meal, my lord,*' we say. '*Do you always eat this well?*'

'No, not always,' confesses Iestyn, 'the wheaten bread is a special treat. We can't grow wheat on our estate because it is too wet and cold. It comes from Anglesey which is much more fertile than Arfon. The bread makes a pleasant change from our usual oats and barley bread.'

'*What is the most important aspect of your farming?*'

'Cattle, of course. No wonder our great-grandfathers used to go on cattle raids. We had an outbreak of cattle disease last year and we were very worried. You see we don't use much money here, and we tend to value things in cows. Oxen are also used to carry loads from place to place and to pull the heavy ploughs. Cattle are very important, and much more valuable than the sheep, pigs and goats we keep.'

'*How do you manage to look after all the animals?*'

'My estate is not very big. It's about 120 acres, and I have 35 workers to help me. Some of them are slaves.'

'*Ah yes, we met the swineherd on the way here.*'

'You met Bleiddud did you? I hope he was doing his work properly. He tends to dream and talk instead of caring for the pigs. He's just one of the slaves here. The rest are villeins.'

'*What is the difference between villeins and slaves?*'

'There's an important difference,' explains Iestyn. 'The villein is a Welshman who can choose for himself as a tenant-farmer what work he does from day to day. Mind you, a villein isn't a free man either. He can't leave his work on the farm and he can never become a poet or a priest or a blacksmith. I often thank God that I was born a free man and into the nobleman's class.'

Hunting and hawking from the Welsh Laws

'*You can enjoy the pleasures of hunting and hawking too, as a nobleman.*'

'Yes, when I have time away from my farming. My great-great-grandfather used to spend a great deal of his time out hunting the stag and wild pig in Snowdonia. I remember my mother singing me a lullaby which described the exciting hunt in the mountains. I can still remember some of it. Let me see:

"When your dad went to hunt,
Spear on his shoulder, a club in his hand,
He called his quick dogs, 'Giff,
Gaff, catch her, catch her, fetch, fetch!'
From a coracle he'd spear
Fish, as a lion strikes a deer.
When your dad went to the mountain
He brought down roebuck,
 wild pig and stag,
A speckled grouse from the mountain tall,
Fish from Derwennydd water fall."'

Everything seems calm and prosperous on this farm in Arfon a thousand years ago. It isn't surprising that when the Prince of Gwynedd, Llywelyn ap Seisyll, died in 1023 the old Welsh chronicle remembered his reign as particularly peaceful and successful. For in his days, it says, 'the whole country (of Gwynedd) was full of goods and men, from sea to sea. There doesn't seem to be any poor or any one in need in all his lands, and no township was empty or unfruitful.'

Index